11 22
STRAND PRICE
5 00

Lives We Carry with Us

ALSO BY ROBERT COLES FROM THE NEW PRESS

Minding the Store: Great Writing About Business, from Tolstoy to Now (co-edited with Albert LaFarge)

A Life in Medicine: A Literary Anthology (co-edited with Randy Testa)

Growing Up Poor: A Literary Anthology (co-edited with Randy Testa and Michael Coles)

Lives We
Carry with Us

Profiles of Moral Courage

Robert Coles

Edited by David D. Cooper

THE NEW PRESS

NEW YORK
LONDON

© 2010 by Robert Coles
All rights reserved.
No part of this book may be reproduced, in any form,
without written permission from the publisher.

Requests for permission to reproduce selections from this
book should be mailed to: Permissions Department,
The New Press, 38 Greene Street, New York, NY 10013.

Published in the United States by The New Press, New York, 2010
Distributed by Perseus Distribution

LIBRARY OF CONGRESS CATALOGING-IN-PUBLICATION DATA

Coles, Robert.
Lives we carry with us : profiles of moral courage / Robert Coles ;
edited by David D. Cooper.
p.   cm.
ISBN 978-1-59558-502-8 (hc. : alk. paper)
1. Courage.   I. Cooper, David D.   II. Title.
BJ1533.C8.C65   2010
920.009'04—dc22
[B]   2010016059

The New Press was established in 1990 as a not-for-profit alternative to the
large, commercial publishing houses currently dominating the book publishing
industry. The New Press operates in the public interest rather than for private
gain, and is committed to publishing, in innovative ways, works of educational,
cultural, and community value that are often deemed insufficiently profitable.

www.thenewpress.com

Composition by dix!
This book was set in Adobe Caslon

Printed in the United States of America

2   4   6   8   10   9   7   5   3   1

For America's children, past, present, and future

Their story, yours and mine—it's what we all carry with us on this trip we take, and we owe it to each other to respect our stories and learn from them.

—William Carlos Williams

CONTENTS

INTRODUCTION
AND EDITOR'S NOTE

David D. Cooper

B eginning in 1970 with an engaging in-depth portrait of psychoanalyst and historian Erik Erikson in the pages of the *New
Yorker* and cresting, most recently, with a compelling book-length
sketch of rock icon and songwriter Bruce Springsteen, the biographical profile has become Robert Coles's signature genre—a staple of
this Pulitzer Prize–winning author's literary life. In this medium,
Coles has found a way to chronicle the lives and honor the influences
of teachers and mentors, writers and artists, the famous along with
ordinary women and men, young and old, to whom Coles listened
over decades of documentary fieldwork around the globe.

The profile is a catalytic genre that cross-fertilizes Coles's unique
gifts: the interpretive dexterity of a renowned psychiatrist, the ob-
servational skills of an influential documentarian; a great teacher's
empathic sensitivity; and, not least, the moral rectitude of a person
who has witnessed firsthand the rough edges of our contemporary
life. Gathered here for the first time, these portraits remind us that
Coles has lived his ideas in the company of others—on the ground
and not just in his head as an academic spectator. The biographical
profile also gives him the latitude and breathing room to explore the
elusive subject of "moral courage," something he refuses to distill
into a tidy definition or reduce to the equations of social science, and

yet has spent a lifetime pursuing, studying, teaching, and writing about in more than eighty books.

Lives We Carry with Us amounts, in effect, to a group portrait of those who have journeyed with Robert Coles from his earliest days as a Harvard undergraduate to his current active retirement in his family home in Concord, Massachusetts. The gallery includes familiar companions such as poet/physician William Carlos Williams and novelist Walker Percy, another fellow physician and spiritual comrade. Some, such as Dorothy Day, offered Coles perspective and encouragement as he wrestled with early misgivings over his medical education. Others, including Erik Erikson and Anna Freud, inspired Coles with purpose as he took his first career steps into child psychiatry. Equally important are those whose lives and writings showed Coles how to move against the grain of convention and authority, figures such as Flannery O'Connor and Dietrich Bonhoeffer. Or Bruce Springsteen and Dorothea Lange, whose art and vision speak to the majesty of ordinary lives that Coles might have entirely bypassed if not for a song sung and recorded or a picture taken and published. The mercurial writer James Agee and the inscrutable philosopher Simone Weil combust with an intense self-scrutiny that Coles found irresistible, terrifying, and necessary. Very old and very young ones, including the morally precocious Ruby Bridges and Delores Garcia—a wise woman of many years, an *anciana*—both had lessons to teach Coles about moral courage in the face of less than ideal circumstances and odds.

Dr. Coles and I collaborated closely in choosing this cross section of thirteen extraordinary lives he has carried with him these past six decades. While we could have invited many, many more to join this select cadre, Dr. Coles is comfortable with the company he keeps here. The difficult editing decisions required in making these selections and editing down what, in some cases, were book-length treatments into relatively brief essays were driven by the inevitable push and pull between practicality and comprehensiveness. My solution, in some cases, has been to draw upon Coles's shorter prose—articles, columns, chapters, essays, prefaces, epilogues, etc.—and assemble what I call "ensemble profiles." I attempted to edit these together as seamlessly as possible. Elsewhere I drew upon longer monograph-length works—for example, Coles's book on Dorothea Lange or his hefty introduction to a selection of Dietrich Bonhoeffer's writings—and picked up certain narrative lines while dropping others.

Within each portrait, I have indicated a change to a different publication with an ornament in the text. Otherwise, I have avoided any conventional editing marks—ellipses, for example, or brackets—that might interrupt narrative flow. On rare occasions, I have had to reintroduce a proper noun or name after cutting a long stretch of original text, but I have not inserted any clarifying or contextual language of my own. My goal has been to create reinvigorated portraits and assemble them into an entirely new and stand-alone book that has its own narrative arc. The only piece included here in its original version is "Una Anciana," one of Dr. Coles's favorite profiles and a fine example of documentary prose. We have had to make compromises along the way—and, with them no doubt, I may unwittingly have introduced mistakes of editorial judgment and practice, for which I apologize.

Each of the portraits collected in *Lives We Carry with Us* folds together the literary gifts that Robert Coles brings to his portrait writing: biographical storytelling, intellectual/interpretive analysis, and personal reflection. In short, these profiles fuse together biography, criticism, and memoir. They offer penetrating examination and usable insight into contemporary lives of moral courage. Taken together, they are Robert Coles's paean to his kinships, a memoir of those guardian spirits who shaped, challenged, and inspired an earnest moral voice of our era.

Lives We Carry with Us

I.

Teachers and Mentors

Erik H. Erikson

In 1961 my wife, Jane, and I were living in Vinings, Georgia, then a small rural community to the northwest of fast-growing Atlanta. Each weekday, Monday through Friday, we visited one or another of the four high schools whose students, white and African American, had begun going to classes together—the onset of court-ordered desegregation. After school, we went to one or two homes, there to talk with particular youths, and their parents, about how a very tense climate of fear and suspicion was coming to bear on their lives, not to mention those of other classmates, and, too, the lives of their teachers. I was then a thirty-year-old child psychiatrist, only recently done with my training; and, quite frankly, I wasn't at all sure that what I was doing had any real use or significance for me, let alone for the young men and women whom I was getting to know as a doctor from up north who had stumbled into the South's school desegregation crisis out of an accident, rather than as part of a planned research effort.

I had entered the Air Force in 1958, under the old doctor's draft, and been sent to Biloxi, Mississippi, where for two years I worked at Keesler Air Force base as a military psychiatrist. I often went into nearby New Orleans to attend medical meetings at Tulane's School of Medicine and conferences at the New Orleans Psychoanalytic

Institute. So doing, I had to make my way through that old port city's streets—and one day found such a journey to be difficult indeed. Street crowds were everywhere, some of them become riotous mobs, intent on blocking the entry of the six-year-old African American children assigned to two elementary schools by officials complying reluctantly with a federal judge's orders, rather than approaching a crisis with sincere helpfulness. As I got to know the young people involved, and the adults who were running the schools, I began to wonder whether I was learning much of any value to anyone—I had started out as an accidental observer, then had taken pains to meet some of the children and others who were attending a troubled city's schools.

My wife and I had moved to Atlanta in an effort to learn more—to find out how desegregation worked for high schoolers who were more inclined to speak readily, and to be more immediately forthcoming to Jane and me than the first graders we'd met and come to know in New Orleans (though years later, the drawings and paintings of those youngsters would prove of lasting instructional value). In both Louisiana and Georgia, for all my experience in pediatrics, then adult and child psychiatry, I began to feel at loose ends, if not at a decided loss. My friends and colleagues of medical school and residency days were now busy in hospitals, outpatient clinics, offices, developing careers for themselves, and my wife's former teaching associates were busy at work in the Boston high school where she had taught, and there we were, not only asking children how their school lives were going, but wondering what these informal, home visits were teaching us—and to what purpose in our decidedly unconventional working lives. We had no institutional base, no office, no research design or proposal to implement, no salary, even. We were drawing on our savings, in a region we'd only begun to know and understand, and we had no conferences or seminars to attend (with all the personal and professional support they offer).

One day Jane and I went to the Vinings post office, and thereafter back home, started sorting the mail (which the postmistress, mischievously once called our "Yankee letters"—as if from a distant country of some notoriety). One envelope stood out—it had Harvard University on the outside, a school Jane and I knew as one-time students. The writer identified himself as a teacher there, and explained the reason for his writing to us: he had heard through a mutual friend, a young historian also teaching at the college, that we were getting to know some of the children who had initiated school desegregation, and that we were also involved with what was soon to be known as the sit-in efforts of SNCC, the Student Non-Violent Coordinating Committee, an aspect of the civil rights struggle then spreading across the states of the Old Confederacy. The writer asked this: "Might we one day meet?" He offered a phone number, and expressed his strong interest in what was happening across Dixie—"of importance to all of us," was a phrase used: one that Jane and I would keep in mind for its quietly affirmative tone. In no time, we were back to our daily, home-visiting routines, and the letter we had received left our consciousness, which had impressions and facts aplenty to retain and try to understand.

One late afternoon, upon our return to our apartment, we heard the phone ringing, and Jane answered it. The caller identified himself as "Professor Erikson," said he taught at Harvard College, and asked whether he had the right number for Jane and me, who (he was told through a mutual friend) were "studying desegregation in Louisiana and Georgia." Yes, we were the ones, Jane said, and then an invitation: were we ever up north, and near Cambridge, Massachusetts, might we meet? Yes, Jane said, though with no great enthusiasm or conviction—nor had we any idea when such a visit would take place (the question had been asked).

Eventually, Jane and I did go north on a visit to our families, and on that occasion we did get to see Professor Erikson—we met him for a cup of coffee, took a walk with him, and even then heard him express gratitude for being able to teach and get to know college students; but we also heard him criticize much of the academic life he had, for the first time, come to witness firsthand. Memorably, he said this: "The young people teach Joan and me a lot—but there is more than enough snobbery here, I'm afraid." So much there, right off (we would later realize) that tells of Erikson—his mention of his wife, Joan, as a spokesperson as well as a companion, and his disdain for a well-known university's version of pomp and circumstance. Indeed, I recall so well the time he took me to the Harvard faculty club for lunch. We were standing in a line, waiting to be seated, and there was plenty to hear—professors talking about this or that. The language was fairly academic, and I did take silent note of it, with no great pleasure; but Erik smiled broadly—and then this: "When you folks finish your work down South, taking on arrogance, you might do some work up here, in places like this." After those words, a shrug of his shoulders, and a shake of his head—as if to emphasize physically, quite personally, what he was hearing and observing with considerable dislike.

The students, though, were a big reward for him, gave him lots to ponder, as he prepared his weekly lectures for them in his "Human Development" course, which took its participants through his well-known "life cycle," which he sometimes playfully pronounced as if it had wheels and was meant to carry willing riders. I have seen many professors at ease with students, but never quite with the eager attentiveness Erik offered them. "I learn so much from them," he once remarked—rarely a refrain to be heard in the buildings he was then frequenting for the giving of lectures, or for a meal now and then. He also followed the students elsewhere; he dined with them, took walks with them, received a steady stream of them during his office hours. Often the students came in pairs, the young men and women a youthful echo of the professor whose wife was constantly there—at his lectures or walking with him, strolling together affectionately across a campus. "I've never met or even seen any of the wives of any of my professors," one student told me—and then this: "Erikson is different." The young woman added this: "His wife is with him all the time—and when she's not there, he keeps mentioning her."

So much to that offhand observation, I would gradually realize, as I got to know Erik better. His ideas, his writing, always passed Joan's attentive, knowing muster—even as she was the one who persuaded him to leave the tight-knit Viennese psychoanalytic community that he'd inadvertently entered as a teacher of children whose parents had come from the world over to see Freud and his colleagues (including his daughter Anna, who spotted young Erik Homburger at work with schoolchildren and suggested he study psychoanalysis with her—a big chapter in Erik's life).

There would be, of course, for Erik and Joan, other important moments, decisions, initiatives, considerations and reconsiderations. Erik was never a lockstep careerist—he was constantly surprising even himself, let alone others. I recall him, in his sixties and seventies, going back to times of decision in his life, as he tried to make sense of how he became the person he then was. In a sense, he was putting to words a particular life's gradual emergence, formation: "It's a mystery, how we become the people we become! I never went to college—I was a high school dropout, in today's language, and now I'm called a professor here. I was an artist, who stumbled into a teaching job and then into 'The Freud Circle,' they were called. Then I met Joan, a Canadian studying in Europe—and lo and behold, I became an American! Talk about luck—though you have to be ready, I'll admit, when luck comes and knocks on your door: ready to say yes, I'll take a chance!

"You ask me to describe myself with an adjective or two [I was then working on a *New Yorker* profile of him, and had wondered aloud how he might speak of his own life—the emergence of the 'identity' of the person who made so very much of that word—gave it so many layered meanings]. Well, I guess I'll hesitate, and end up wandering all over the map with avowals and disclaimers! But if I had to limit myself to a few words, I'd say that I was restless, maybe a bit rebellious, always one who looked and looked, then listened closely. I can tell that I'm hedging my bets here, psychologically, as we all do, so often; but let's settle for 'restless,' not as an element of

psychopathology (who is without some of that!)—but as an eagerness to keep exploring (again: looking and looking). Here I'd better
stop, leave it as it is, the subject of my subjectivity!"

Vintage Erikson, I then thought—his constant effort to circle
around things, and thereby take their fullest, widest measure. What
a tape recorder can't document, however, is the speaker's bodily posture, facial expressions, as he has his say. Erik was circling around
himself, so to speak, he was testing things with his arms, sometimes
his right, sometimes his left, sometimes pointing, sometimes moving his hand up or down or sideways—an artist at work, I remember thinking, looking carefully, the upper limbs painting away, with
language as the medium, in this case, of the speaker's self-expression
(even as the hands were moving to convey a life's vigorous mobility).

In 1964, I went with Erik and Joan to Mississippi—he was working on his Gandhi book, and he wanted to witness the nonviolent
efforts of American students to challenge the bastion of segregation, some of them former members of his college class. Erik was
ever wanting to see and see, then move on—so as to see more, learn
more, know more: a memorable demonstration of energetic engagement with people, with a place, with so much history that was then
unfolding. I remember exhaustion setting in—all of us needing a
break from a hectic, demanding, and troubling day's documentary
work (so much to hear and see). But Erik was unflagging, always
eager to add more to the growing store of sights and sounds that had
come our way, even as Joan and I suggested a pause here and there!
"Yes," he turned to me once, as he looked with obvious admiration
at what some young Americans had accomplished—the building of
a school and clinic for needy children; and then this: "So much to
witness here—history in the making, people building their future."
Those words, I realized, were Erik's way of describing not only
others at work but his own life's work, his relentless insistence that
childhood be understood, that a society be observed, that the deeds
of those who enter history be put on the record—the why's of their
personal lives become instruments of history's march forward, all

told the rest of us by Erik the artist become psychoanalyst, become teacher, become writer, become biographer and historian. Such a presence, his, such a presence, Joan's, such a joint presence, theirs, many of us fondly remember, and still sorely miss!

Of Freud's children, his youngest, Anna (born in 1895, just as he was developing his views on dreams, on the unconscious as a harbinger of their expression), was the only one to follow her father's steps and become a psychoanalyst. She witnessed firsthand those first decades of a profession's emergence—the years in which her father risked professional isolation and the scorn of various others, including those in universities and churches. And she saw how he methodically, tenaciously built a world around him, with patients and students and colleagues informally gathered, some from nearby, but more and more, as word of his work spread, some from afar.

I well knew Erikson had once been an analysand of Anna Freud's. I knew, too, that because of what Anna and her father were trying to do in Vienna during the 1920s, when young Erik Homburger (Homburger was his stepfather's name) arrived, his life would most decidedly and dramatically change—he would find his future occupation, and he would find a love that culminated in marriage. It was a privilege, an eye-opening visit for me, to hear Anna Freud talk about a fellow child psychoanalyst of hers who had once been her analysand. Erikson had been her student in the courses she gave at the Vienna Psychoanalytic Institute—and by then (the early 1970s) this distinguished, even renowned writer and teacher, whose books had greatly influenced thousands of Americans, had become a professor at Harvard University, where (I well knew) the students took to him with great enthusiasm. (And we should keep in mind that his writing forged unprecedented insights into growing up in America, even if he came here when he was just over thirty, and not as a fluently speaking visitor.)

Yet again, though, Miss Freud was worried about perspective—

mine, of course, and maybe that of others: "I know that here in the States [she spoke as the Englishwoman she had become] you all know Erik Erikson (how do you say it—he has become a 'household name'!). I'm not sure that many realize how his life became what it is, and that's his main interest (isn't it!): 'identity,' how we become the individuals, the men or women we know ourselves to be, and others recognize—well, as *us*. I remember him as a man in his twenties. He came to us through his childhood friend, Peter Blos [who also became a child psychoanalyst]. We had begun a school for the children of those who had come to Vienna to see my father—many were Americans. By then my father and his books were widely known, especially in America—and it was a riddle to him (perhaps 'irony' is the correct word here), because he was no 'fan,' as Americans would put it, of the States. I recall him saying: 'I don't understand that country,' and then he smiled, and added: 'I don't understand why they have turned toward us [his theories] faster than anywhere!' He had come here [in 1916], and your foremost psychologist, William James, had greeted him warmly, but he never sensed any overwhelming enthusiasm, and I think he had misread a country then—maybe still—hard for many of us in Europe to figure out. You need to know history—for a long while, I know, people came to America to settle it, but among the professional classes in Europe, there was no interest in going to America, whereas Americans who were doctors or professors or writers came to Europe.

"Maybe I'm above my neck here, and am in trouble, but when the Nazis seized power in Germany, it wasn't as easy for some of us to think of quickly leaving Austria or Germany [where some psychoanalysts lived, especially in Berlin] for North America. In fact, Erik was the first in our Vienna world to want to leave for America [in the early 1930s, after Hitler's ascension as chancellor, in 1933] and we did wonder why—but his wife was from Canada, and had gone to college in New York City, I recall [at Barnard]. They were wise to leave, and lucky to be able to go there, we now readily say, but I wondered when they left what they'd do. He had become a talented teacher, first, and then he learned to be a psychoanalyst with us, but he had not gone to college, or any professional [graduate] school, and I do recall wondering whether he'd be able to find a job, make a living—[he had] no 'credentials,' as you say, and child psychoanalysis had yet to become an established (or 'regular') profession.

"I remember asking Erik, 'What will you do, and where will you go to do it?' I had in mind that maybe he'd find a job as a teacher, and get to work psychoanalytically with some children—what he'd begun doing here with us. He put his hand through his hair (a frequent gesture of his, he used to think, to admit some anxiety, or better, uncertainty) and then he said: 'We'll find our way, we just will.' He spoke in German, but he was beginning to speak in English with the help of Joan, and that was what did happen: he found his way and he became an American, 'with all his might' is how I put it when I think about the new life he started here, becoming one of this country's writers—who explained what he'd learned from us in his very own way, I think it fair to say."

She was, with those last words, getting close to a designation or approximation of her former analysand's "new life," its nature and purpose. Erik and Joan Erikson did, indeed, leave Vienna for America in 1933, and soon enough he was living in Massachusetts, then Connecticut, then California, and back East, in Massachusetts—a child psychoanalyst who knew well how to work with children and young people so commonly called adolescents or teenagers. He taught his newly acquired discipline in colleges, took part in seminars, took on patients. He carried a substantial clinical load at the Austen Riggs Center in Stockbridge, Massachusetts, and right away impressed academic psychologists such as Henry A. Murray, at Harvard, and the doctors who worked at Yale's Child Study Center. In California, he became a noteworthy part of the San Francisco Psychoanalytic Institute, and gloried, I think it fair to say, in the invitations of America's West, an open vitality that he found engaging, even as he couldn't help being drawn to a landscape of great and often surprising beauty. In New England, of course, he was a bit closer to Europe and its proud intellectuality, though a wry sense of humor and the part of him that had never experienced the routines and rituals of academic life gave him a certain immunity from the professorial self-assurance he encountered in well-known universities. In Vienna he had been a layman rather than a physician-psychiatrist among the Freud circle—like Anna Freud herself, who had also managed to avoid the educational hurdles that for young Erik Erikson were distinctly uninviting. "He was a loner, and his very own person, not easily fitted into the usual classification," Miss Freud observed, and then her shrewd attempt at the evaluation of national character—a version, really, of Erikson's interest in that subject: "I think he found a home in America that he'd not had in Europe—once in 'the States' he could be welcomed as a person who wasn't attached to 'the old country,' and was very anxious to turn this 'new land' into the home he'd been seeking, and at last had found."

She went on to speak of Erikson's "*Wanderjahr*," which he had mentioned often, even worked into the last introduction he wrote to *Childhood and Society* (1985). Even then, perhaps, as he wandered through fields and forests, he was learning intuitively about the word "identity," the phrase "identity crisis." He would later use these words again and again as a writing psychoanalyst, ever determined to explain the complexities, psychological and social, that come the way of young people in their attempts (sometimes their painful struggles) to "grow up," meaning find their place in a particular town, nation, and time. What I have just stated may seem unexceptional, even obvious to some readers—yet that was often Erikson's purpose: to connect the depths of psychoanalytic inquiry and awareness to the surface, even homespun knowledge we all acquire as we enter, then go through our lives. No question, for instance, many youths have to contend with their wishes and desires as they pass the muster of their consciences, seek expression, fulfillment, in human connections of one kind or the other. Still, such a time in a young man's, a young woman's life occurs in one place, in one decade of one century; hence the mooring a youth feels as one tied, deep down, to a family, a religion, a neighborhood, a contemporary world with its demands, requests, requirements, values, assertions and, too, the bearings a youth finds as he or she decides to head here or there in an effort to find direction—to get some realized sense of meaning with respect to human existence, its purpose and significance.

No wonder, then, a psychoanalyst whose ancestry was Danish, but who lived in Germany, then learned a profession in Austria, only to come to the United States with a Canadian-born wife, and see his three children, two sons and a daughter, become Americans, would develop a strong interest in the way psychology intersects with sociology, culture and nationalism, history. No wonder, too, a man who had in his background Judaism and Protestantism, and who was a child during the First World War, a parent during the Second World War, and saw the continent that was home to his ancestors, immediate as well as distant, turn into a region of fear and hate, even murder, despite the so-called "advancement," the richness of tradition, to be found there—it is truly no surprise that such a person would give great thought to the effect events in the world at large have on many of us, no matter the private or personal aspects of our particular lifetime. When Freud titled one of his most broadly and philosophically searching books *Civilization and Its Discontents*, he was sending an implicit signal to his colleagues that Erikson, more than any of them, maybe, was prepared by his fate to receive, reflect upon, how our worries and times of unrest tell us a lot about who we are, where we live, and, very important, what we have learned to uphold, regard as decisively valuable. We fall short, quiver with "phobias," "anxieties" (those oft-used clinical words!) that have their origins not only in our family life (all those "complexes" which psychoanalysis has submitted to this century!), but in the town, the time that is our own to claim but that, not rarely, exerts its authority upon us.

Those of us fortunate enough to know and work with Erikson the teacher, and share with him as would-be or about-to-be clinical observers, often heard him talk quite directly about the personal interests and theoretical claims that characterize his writing. I well recall, in that regard, a seminar in which Erikson, as leader, talked at great length of Freud—the story, as it were, that prompted and informed books such as *Group Psychology and the Analysis of the Ego* and *Moses and Monotheism*. Yes, the former book summoned Freud's interest in the mind and its workings; the latter book similarly explored the complicated and extensive origins of the "Super-Ego," of religiously transmitted oughts and naughts that become for so many of us lifelong mandates, sources of alarm and foreboding and regret or remorse. But for Erikson such an occasion was not only one for psychoanalytic rumination, speculation, but rather for a broad discussion, as he was wont to put it, of "the relationship between ideas and historical actuality as it influences them." (I have pages of notes with those foregoing words on them.) Freud was intent, always, on tracing the sources of our troubles, and he did so as a psychological archaeologist, ever ready to go back across the years, ascertain what happened when, and why, and with which consequences. His main cast of characters for any patient's drama were the parents, the siblings: the family counts in our continuing effort to make do with life—our memories of early family years and our later arrangements with others as a repetition of that past, an echo faint or loud. As he grew older, Freud held to his original concepts, paradigms, but he also lived to see himself and his family put in great possible danger: Hitler's rise to power and all that it would mean for millions, certainly including the entire Freud family. When his daughter Anna was taken into custody by the Gestapo, he knew he had best depart Austria immediately, if at all possible. And lucky for him, he and his wife and children were let out, though not his sisters, who eventually perished in a concentration camp. But he already knew what was ahead, well before the Nazis entered Vienna, and so in the book on group psychology he was trying to comprehend what comes over presumably well-educated and reasonable people when they became part of a crowd (a group), if not a racist or political mob—and when he contemplated Moses, his fate, he was seeking to know what it means to be a proud people, singled out by God in their own estimate of their history, and so resented by others.

Here is Anna Freud looking back—and referring to her father in a way Erikson would, were he then present to make the case: "My father was horrified by what was happening in Germany [in the 1920s and 1930s], and he began to wonder why people give way to craziness that goes beyond psychiatric—even psychoanalytic—conceptualization: the madness of mobs, and the scapegoating that can get going when social violence runs through a society. That is what Erik Erikson helped us all realize—as he put it: 'childhood,' even that, is connected to 'society'; and all of us adults, supposedly 'mature,' can fall prey to an irrationality that belongs to the mob, but the mob, as Erikson would remind us, is set in motion by the 'society,' and by 'history'—there you have his important contribution to our [psychoanalytic] thinking."

I could imagine Erikson's grateful ears tingling were he to hear such a compliment from his analyst and teacher. But he knew, anyway, what he had striven hard to recognize as he roamed America, and he realized that he had developed his own take on Freud and his work, on psychoanalysis and its possibilities, its occasional limits, as a mode of introspection and human connectedness. He became, by 1950, when *Childhood and Society* was published, and thereafter, as his essays and books appeared, a giant figure both within his profession and in the American academic and cultural world to which he belonged, no matter his lack of formal education, an irony he himself sometimes mentioned. Indeed, when he became, finally, a professor at Harvard he was often ready to leave—claiming an "inability" to adjust to the academic life. He was, in a way, ever the rebel, quick to distance himself from perceived "stuffiness" or proclaimed (and institutionalized) "certainties" (I well recall his use of both words!), which he regarded with skepticism, even alarm.

No wonder, then, he sought human understanding through not only psychoanalysis but the study of history, and of individuals

(Luther and Gandhi) who made a difference in history. All his writing reveals that search, essentially an unashamedly moral one. He searched for "insight," yes, but also for the "responsibility" that such psychological awareness places on us who study and practice psychoanalysis and on the patients who receive its gifts: those who have been given so much must respond to others far less privileged with respect to what they can perceive within themselves and others. All his writing, as well, reveals an urgent effort to sustain psychoanalysis by extending its wisdom to other terrains of reflection. He was an artist as a young man who later became an artist as a psychoanalyst—he called upon religious traditions and historical learning in such a way that he could contemplate ambiguities and paradoxes and contradictions, rather than try to banish them in the name of theoretical absolutism. Not least, he was a marvelously interesting and compelling storyteller, who made the English language his own, savored its evocative and dramatic invitations, and thereby drew to his wise words countless interested (and needy) students, readers, fans: a master of clinical observation who avoided the reductive mannerisms of the clinic, and so doing, became a spirited emissary of the Dr. Freud whose ideas helped Erik H. Erikson become, in turn, a spokesman for, an interpreter of, those ideas, and maybe, in his own vigorous, knowing manner, a lifesaver of them, one who ensured their continued and meaningful presence among so many of us.

In late February 1970, I returned to Mississippi with Erik and Joan Erikson. We went first to Leake County, to a settlement called Harmony. I had been there before, knew the people. In 1964 I had watched them build a community center for themselves. They would build by day, and by night stand guard over their growing "project." Klansmen came and came but were fought off. Shots were fired, homes and churches dynamited, but men with rifles kept that center from harm. The people of Harmony are black yeoman farmers.

They are proud landowners, sturdy and tough Mississippians. They
are not about to leave the state, not about to stop planting, stop harvesting, stop praying, stop fighting for something. For what are they
fighting? They ask themselves that, but not in order to come up with
stock answers, half-meant banalities, or overcomplicated analyses of
life's "meaning." They want their children to live, to have a doctor
or dentist when needed, to have enough food every day, to attend
schools where "the teachers be respectful to the boys and girls, and
really teach and don't squelch them and squeeze all the juices out of
them."

We talked with some of those children; they were three or four
or five years old and taking part in a Head Start program. We also
talked with teachers and with parents. The children were naturally
quiet at first, wide-eyed with intense curiosity. Erikson noticed their
eyes, how they kept upon us, held to us, pursued us. He also noticed
the energy and enthusiasm of the children, many spared hunger,
malnutrition and a whole range of diseases, if not death itself, by the
good food and medical care Head Start provides. He sat down with
a group of children and soon was drawing for them—horses and
cars. The boys and girls looked and looked. They looked at the artist, looked at his pictures, back and forth. Later in the day we all sat
around in a circle and the women of Harmony, teachers and mothers
both, followed us and one another with their eyes, and talked and
talked and talked. We heard of the hardships they knew and still
know, but we also heard of their fierce determination to persist, to
achieve things, tangible and intangible, things that in sum amount
to "life, liberty and the pursuit of happiness." It was not always easy,
not easy to hear the stories of violence, murder, extreme hardship.
Nor was it easy to answer the questions about children, about how
they grow, what they do and do not notice and believe as they get
older and older. Quietly Erik and Joan Erikson responded, told the
women what they are now trying to do—in fact, find the answers to
some of those questions, find out how children in India and Paki-
stan or ghetto children in American cities or our middle-class white

children or children on our Indian reservations and even our rural black children all come to look at themselves and their world. The Eriksons, working with Mrs. Arthur Penn, are doing so by asking children to use certain toys, build things, and then talk about a little world they choose to create. They are doing so not to "get data," to "find" something, but rather to see, to be shown—by children who are simply given a chance to play, to imagine, to exercise the will.

The people of Harmony asked the Eriksons to come back, and not only out of routine politeness. And in the Delta other parents and children were no less interested, no less curious, no less hospitable. We moved across a wide arc of the Delta, through Yazoo City, through Louise, through Midnight and Belzoni. We stopped at various Head Start centers. We visited with children and their teachers. We talked with the children. We listened to them sing. We watched them play. We were fed good food. And toward the end of our stay, as we drove along, past cotton fields and the cotton gins, past the cabins, past the little Delta towns that in a flash appear and disappear, I noticed Erik Erikson looking out the window, observing—but in his face also responding, trying hard to make sense of what he saw, and just as important, trying hard to learn what he believed, where his ethical concerns would require him to go. I reminded myself that he needn't have been there, needn't have been in that car, on the particular road; yet he had wanted to be there, had come there. I reminded myself that he was getting old, that he was perhaps tired. But a few moments later he was no longer tired; he had napped briefly and so was wide awake. I thought of a line in Robert Penn Warren's *Audubon*: "He walked in the world. Knew the lust of the eye." I thought of a line in T.S. Eliot's "East Coker": "Old men ought to be explorers." Then we came upon yet another fork in the road, and there was no more time for thoughts. We had to decide where we were going next, and by God, hope we would find our way there.

Anna Freud

In 1950, while an undergraduate at Harvard College, I chanced upon a lecture given by Anna Freud. On my way "home" (to my dormitory room) from the organic chemistry laboratory, which for me at the time seemed a parcel of hell's acreage, I met another pre-medical student who was already interested in psychiatry and psychoanalysis as well. He knew of the scheduled lecture and suggested we grab a Coke, then hurry for good seats—for there was certain, he said, to be a large audience to hear Miss Freud. I had to confess that I didn't know who Miss Freud was—except that she must be some kin to Sigmund Freud, none of whose books I had read. My friend, on the other hand, knew a great deal about her and her father, and while we had our snack—in Hayes Bickford, a cafeteria long gone—he told me some of what he knew.

I still remember one sentence—the sheer innocence of it, in retrospect!—and I remember becoming more, rather than less, confused for hearing it: "She discovered child psychoanalysis." What did he mean by "discovery"? I asked. (He and I were getting our fill, then, of scientific discoveries—all the laboratory breakthroughs Professor Louis Fieser recounted in his lectures and in his daunting organic chemistry textbook.) My friend was short on details. He didn't know how "she had done it," but she was the one, he asserted, who "brought" psychoanalysis to the nursery. When I asked how in the world such analytic inquiry took place, I was told that if I went to the lecture I'd surely find my answer. By then I had the sense to lose interest, although as I did my friend made one of those cautionary remarks I'd later find familiar: "Don't be scared by what she'll say." I hadn't the slightest idea what that remark meant—or more properly, was meant to mean. I can still remember my puzzled interest in what seemed to me a mix of solicitude and barely concealed condescension. While stifling the urge to pursue the matter, I also put aside the impulse to say good-bye, go study chemistry rather than listen to Miss Freud's lecture. I realized that such a decision, whatever its basis, would be seen only as a confirmation that I was, indeed, a bit frightened. In self-defense, I showed a heightened interest in both Freuds while we made haste to get to the lecture hall early.

We sat fairly close to the front. While we were waiting, we looked around at the others, and noticed that many, indeed most of them, weren't our age, weren't students at all. In the 1950s, the "New Lecture Hall" was much used (it is now in great need of repair). In those days, attendance was taken at the beginning of each class, so I would ordinarily have sat in an assigned seat. It seemed doubly strange, then, to be sitting where I wished, and to be among so many "adults." Quite a few spoke in accents, and I was not always able to fathom the meaning of many words used by those who did speak excellent English. My friend observed my perplexity, hastened to help me out: we were in the midst of the "psychoanalytic community." Again I didn't ask him what he meant for fear of being thought stupid; but I was not at all reassured. I knew next to nothing then about psychiatry or psychoanalysis, only that Sigmund Freud was someone important in twentieth-century cultural or intellectual history, someone who had figured out how the mind works, what dreams meant, and a way of helping people who had gotten into psychological trouble. The phrase "psychoanalytic community," for an instant, at least, conjured in my mind the thought of a somewhat disturbed group of people— maybe "patients" who lived in Cambridge and had been treated by this or that psychiatrist and who now wanted to hear a prominent one speak. Years later, of course, lying on the couch and letting all things come to mind, into words, I would recall my ignorance that afternoon—a twenty-year-old brought up by a devoutly religious mother from an Iowa farm and an English-born scientist father with little interest in or patience for the social sciences, never mind, to use Freud's word, matters "metapsychological." I would also recall the nature of that historical moment—the years immediately after the Second World War, when psychoanalysis was just beginning to have an influence on American culture. But at the time, all I could try to do was to appear as sophisticated as possible—listening to my friend without evident surprise or anxiety as he told me about where "they tended to live," to have their offices, and even their fees: the astonishing sum of ten or fifteen dollars an hour for five visits a week, for years. In the privacy of my mind I wondered who had so much money, and why so many visits each week. Wasn't one good long talk enough to help anyone fathom what ailed him or her?

Soon such thoughts were interrupted by the arrival on the platform of a short, thin, middle-aged lady, accompanied by a taller, somewhat heavyset man. I never did, even back then, catch his name. He introduced Miss Freud briefly, and she wasted no time getting into the heart of her message—an exposition of the important principles of psychoanalysis, its view of mental function, and its clinical method. To my surprise, I followed her line of reasoning rather well. Here was someone who really wanted to teach us; who spoke with conviction and clarity; who did not intimidate or condescend to her audience. I didn't, of course, use such words back then. Less exact psychologically, I simply pronounced the lecture "good," the speaker "persuasive." I admitted to being "interested" in what she had said—and told my friend I intended to go to the library and look up what she had written. Since I was heavily burdened with course work, such a decision was a real commitment.

At the time, I was also involved as a volunteer tutor in what was still called a "settlement house"—a place where children from vulnerable families (psychologically or sociologically speaking) received needed educational or medical assistance. I remember even today the first visit I made to that settlement house after Miss Freud's lecture. I was working with Gerry, a nine- or ten-year-old boy who had severe temper tantrums in school and had been suspended for a week or longer. He and I studied his homework together, and I often brought him a candy bar. I had assumed that his primary problem was medical—he had a "clubfoot" that gave him difficulty as he tried to get to school, play with his friends, keep up with the rhythms of his neighborhood. Although I knew he had a temper, that seemed of little significance: Gerry never mentioned it to me; I had never observed it; and no one else seemed interested in it; whereas his physical difficulty (and the repeated ear infections he had suffered earlier, necessitating surgery in those years before antibiotics) prompted much discussion. He was seen as a physically handicapped child in need of some help in learning, because he'd missed school when younger and was still somewhat incapacitated.

It is hard now to remember Gerry as I knew him, thought of him, back then. Today so many of us—millions, perhaps, without any idea of who Anna Freud was—will meet or learn of a Gerry, and immediately think not of his body, but of his mind. What happens to a boy's head when his leg does not work well—is congenitally short or abnormal with respect to bone formation, muscular or nerve supply? It was less than forty years ago that Gerry and I did our weekly work together, yet my view of him back then would be regarded by a student volunteer today as naive, indeed. Thanks to Miss Freud's lecture, however, I began to have some second thoughts about Gerry, and my own involvement with him. In her lecture, she had mentioned the impact upon children of illness and deformity—the way in which a child whose body doesn't work well takes the defect to heart. As she spoke, Gerry had momentarily crossed my mind. Now, sitting across the table from Gerry, I saw her before me. I wondered what she would think of this boy, who could be so cooperative, even compliant with me—yet, who would strike out angrily at friends at home, classmates at school, swear without restraint, throw rocks, withdraw in sullen resentment and defiance. No doubt, I imagined, she would say something to the boy—be a good teacher in the sense of knowing le mot juste.

That afternoon, as I sat with Gerry and helped him with a school composition, I had a fantasy that Miss Freud would arrive, ask the boy to come over to her teacher's desk, sit him down in a chair nearby, put him at ease, tell him some things about himself that would have the clear, convincing ring of truth, then send him off, a changed person. How would he be different? I hadn't really thought the matter out, but I suppose I had in mind the image of an attentive student (Gerry) listening to a compelling teacher (Miss Freud) and, as a consequence, *shaping up*—a phrase my father used to use in an admonishing and exhortative fashion. In no time, however, I was caught up again with the immediate contingencies of tutoring, and Miss Freud slipped out of my memory.

A year later I was in medical school, where I fastened my hopes on pediatric work with children. During an internship and residency in pediatrics and child psychiatry, I became especially interested in the ways children struggle with severe illness—their moods, their hopes and worries, as they lay sick in the hospital. It was then that I had occasion to hear Miss Freud again. She had come back to America, and she was now talking about her work after the Second World War with children who had survived concentration camps. This talk was less "public"; it was given in the seminar room of a Boston hospital. I had been invited to attend by an older physician, a surgeon who had taken an interest in psychoanalysis and, as a matter of fact, had been analyzed by a prominent colleague of Anna Freud's father, yet another "refugee" who had found his way during the late 1930s to the United States.

The small room was crowded with about forty people, almost all physicians. I was once more struck by the directness of the speaker, her evident command of her subject, her willingness to share her knowledge with us in such an accessible manner. Each sentence seemed a perfectly formed jewel, sparkling and delightful to contemplate. An uncanny mixture of relaxed self-assurance and intense dedication emanated from this small, still thin woman, plainly dressed, her voice strong but not insistent. I still remember the talk, and I still remember a sudden desire, afterward, to ask a question about a girl I had come to know, a patient at Children's Hospital in Boston. This girl had a serious diabetic condition, and yet seemed so resolutely cheerful and confident that all of us—nurses, social workers, doctors—wondered what "really" crossed the child's mind when she was alone, when she was not putting up such a valiant show of outgoing optimism. I didn't expect Miss Freud to say what our young patient was thinking, but all of us at the hospital were worried about her future psychological prospects, and so I did ask about prognosis—about the likelihood of psychopathology developing in a year, two years, or even farther along.

Even now, I can see as well as hear Miss Freud's response. She put her hands on her papers, moved them slowly, deliberately, but with increasing animation. Her message was pointed—and a real challenge for the young doctors in the audience who were accustomed to receiving categorical or specific advice: "Who can ever foretell what a child will be like in the time ahead?"

I wrote the words down, and found them quite unsatisfying—the kind of remark, actually, one of my grandparents would make out of the stoic surrender of old age. I was convinced that *she* was the very one who could with reliability and accuracy do such prophesying. But she persisted, and reminded us, at length, how difficult it can be for even the best-informed observer of any given child to know what tomorrow will bring in the way of psychological adjustment, or the lack thereof. Later that week, when George Gardner, chief of child psychiatry at the Children's Hospital, and a child psychoanalyst, met with us residents, we discussed Miss Freud's lecture, the way in which she answered questions and, especially, her seeming reluctance to make psychological forecasts. His response was brief: "She is genuinely modest." I think some of us took that comment as a reprimand—so heady were we with our newfound (and incomplete) knowledge, and so eager were we to wield it in front of others, colleagues and patients alike.

Soon afterward I began a prolonged period of supervision with Dr. Gardner, who admired both Miss Freud and another child psychoanalyst whose work I was just then getting to know, Erik H. Erikson. Often when I came to my supervisory hour Dr. Gardner would listen to my case presentation, make a comment or two about the child, or the therapy I was trying to do, and then bring up for discussion some aspect of Anna Freud's thinking, or Erik H. Erikson's. During such talks, we tried to connect the writing of those two child analysts to the clinical issues I had brought to Dr. Gardner's attention. He was a great one for the casual remark that was meant to reassure a nervous young doctor—but often unnerved him. For example, after I'd made my initial presentation, he might say: "I can see why you are concerned, but don't forget your biggest ally: time." Hearing those words, I was supposed to sit back, stretch my legs, and swallow the soft drink or coffee he invariably had waiting for his supervisees.

Dr. Gardner asked me to read carefully Anna Freud's *The Ego and the Mechanisms of Defense*, as well as her monograph *War and Children*. We discussed her point of view at great length; and in this way, she became a distinct and continuing presence all through my supervisory experience as a resident in child psychiatry. In the mid-1930s, she had insisted upon the mind's capacity to respond with energy, guile, resiliency, and, not least, intelligent resourcefulness in response to the unconscious yearnings and compulsions that psychoanalytic theorists had worked so hard to understand. This was so even with young children, Dr. Gardner reminded me, and I learned to see this resilience in the boys and girls I was treating—in their often astonishing maneuvers, remarks, deeds, dreams, drawings, as they tried hard to give their lives shape and purpose, however burdensome their psychological difficulties. "Miss Freud will help you as you work," Dr. Gardner once told me in a moment of reassurance.

Indeed, the sensible directness of her observations on children was a welcome contrast to some of the theoretical writing I was then trying to master in the psychoanalytic journals. His comment—or prophecy—was meant to help me make the connection between clinical challenges and Miss Freud's ideas in such a manner that the children under my care would benefit. It is not always that articles and books have such a bearing on the lives of both doctors and patients.

After completing my training in child psychiatry, I went south to Mississippi under the old doctor's draft law to take charge of a large U.S. Air Force neuropsychiatric hospital. There, in nearby New Orleans, I underwent psychoanalysis and took courses at the Psychoanalytic Institute, while also beginning work with the black (and, eventually, white) children caught in the turmoil of school desegregation. What was to be a two-year stint in Dixie turned into a whole new professional life—an effort to understand how children of various backgrounds manage under all sorts of social, cultural, and political circumstances. I have described that work in a number of books, and in them I constantly make reference to Anna Freud. Indeed, in the very first articles I wrote, in the late 1950s and early 1960s, she was very much *there*—helping me understand the young polio patients I came to know at the Children's Hospital, and later, the beleaguered children of Louisiana who faced down daily mobs in order to integrate elementary schools.

By 1965, I was anxious to study her writing at length and to write about the significance of her ideas for people in my field. I titled the essay "The Achievement of Anna Freud"; it was published in a literary quarterly, *The Massachusetts Review*, in 1966. A month or so later, I received a letter from Miss Freud, thanking me, and saying that I was on target. (An analysand of hers had shown the article to her.) I replied. She replied. We were on our way to a correspondence that lasted for many years, and eventually, to meetings, discussions—many valuable exchanges that helped me in so many ways. Her visits to Yale, for a while an annual occurrence, became an important part of my life—the trip there to meet her, listen to her, learn from her. Child psychoanalysis was far from her only interest. She read broadly, had a lively mind that reached toward the world and its various problems. She was especially interested, during the late 1960s and 1970s, in the social and racial problems with which both the United States and Great Britain were struggling, even as she had responded so brilliantly and passionately to the English children who lived under the threat of Nazi bombers during the Second World War, or to those children who had survived the concentration camps at the end of that war. To talk with her about such matters was always a privilege and moment of important instruction.

To talk with her about other matters—that of religion as children experience it, for instance—was not only a privilege, but also, I now realize, an utter necessity for me as I examined the way the boys and girls I was interviewing saw the world, tried to find meaning in it. Again and again, as I tried to make sense of the research I was doing—the statements I heard, the drawings and paintings I was shown—I thought back to her written remarks, her spoken comments, made as we looked together at a particular child's artwork, read transcripts of the child's declarations, questions, complaints, speculations. We carry with us, emotionally and intellectually, various guardian spirits (or "mentors," as today's language would have it), and for me Anna Freud was one such constant presence.

Still later, when I came to work with, and know, and in time write about Erik H. Erikson, the name of Anna Freud came up: she was his analyst. Then came a friendship with Helen Ross, a child analyst who was close to Miss Freud. Miss Ross and I were on the board of the Field Foundation in the 1970s, and a major interest of that foundation was the training center Miss Freud ran at Hampstead in London. Her reports, her letters, her American visits, meant a lot to us—another chance to learn from her. To read her accounts of how things went at her clinic was to learn not only about a child psychoanalyst's view of the young, but a strong leader's visionary interest in the next generation. So many educators of all kinds (doctors, nurses, social workers, teachers) have taken their training at Hampstead and learned from Miss Freud not only the specifics of psychoanalysis but, more broadly, how to think about the possibilities in children as well as their inevitable times of trial. So many of us have worked with children differently, thought differently, because of her. She was a strong moral and intellectual force in psychoanalysis for a half-century.

During the 1970s, I often thought of writing a biography of Anna Freud, and several times broached the subject with her. She was, indeed, as Dr. Gardner had told us, "genuinely modest." Once, when a mutual friend sent an article I'd written about her, she wrote back to say that I had too high an opinion of her, but that "anyway, it is something to live up to." Instead of a biography, she suggested, "you can do me the honor of using my thoughts in your work." I remember her as she spoke those words in a Yale dormitory: eyes as always alertly focused on the person being addressed, a cup of coffee in her hand, a plate of Viennese cakes nearby. One did not easily take issue with her. On the other hand, she was more than eager to be of help to me as I wrote or considered writing biographical studies of others—Erik Erikson, Simone Weil, Dorothy Day. She even read my essays on William Carlos Williams and Walker Percy, and was intrigued, I think it fair to say, by those two physician-writers. After all, she was the daughter of a predecessor of theirs. Several times, as a matter of fact, she told me how important writing was to her father—not only the ideas formulated, but also the process of giving the words a proper and inviting shape.

I was working on these biographies of Simone Weil and Dorothy Day when Miss Freud died in London in 1982. That twin project (two books written in tandem) took the form it did because of a suggestion she once made to me: "You can highlight their work; you can show the intellectual directions they took; you can weigh and compare their successes and failures." Anyone who knew her would recognize in those words her characteristic way of putting things— clear, pointed, sparse phrasing—and a certain quality of mind as well. In her advice she showed a keen sense of life's victories, life's defeats, as they come upon us all, as well as a wry skepticism that kept company with personal decency, and reticence, shyness almost. She did not suggest that I do a conventional psychological portrait or biography of those two women. Not that they, or Miss Freud herself, wouldn't be fit candidates for such. She and they lived interesting, provocative, even challenging lives. But for her (as for her two fellow inhabitants of the twentieth century), the significance of a life ought to be judged, ultimately, in this way: "What she [Simone Weil] left us to think about is what we *should* be thinking about! We can safely leave aside her personality with no risk of missing something very important and revealing." Again, a characteristic bit of self-revelation—of the ironic outlook that informed so much of her thinking. She was not one to be startled by contemporary outbursts of psychohistorical exuberance. A clinician for many decades, she knew how unsurprising, finally, so much psychopathology turns out to be. No wonder she was interested in what a person *does* with conflict, rather than a continual emphasis on its nature. For instance, on one occasion, a report on a rather disturbed child, a dramatically disturbed child, was presented to her. At the age of thirteen, the boy had set many fires, and spoke in apocalyptic imagery about the imminent end of life on this planet through a nuclear war. Miss Freud shrugged her shoulders and said that the "psychodynamics" were "all too familiar"—but then quickly added: "This boy is determined to let everyone know what is troubling him. He is announcing his problems as if they are accomplishments." An interesting perspective, I thought then, and still do, for a biographer to keep in mind.

⁂

Anna Freud did much to connect psychoanalytic knowledge *about* children (learned from the memories of adults) to psychoanalytic work *with* children. So much of the understanding today's child psychiatrists possess was enabled by the work she did for over half a century with boys and girls troubled by virtue of their experiences in particular families, or as a consequence of the Nazi air assaults on London during World War II, or, horror of horrors, as a result of living in concentration camps during that same war. To such children Miss Freud, as she was called by so many of us for so long, gave all she had: a brilliant, knowing mind; enormous, unflagging patience; and the consummate skill she had as a clinician—able, I often noted, to get to the heart of the matter with a child, with his or her parents, in what struck the rest of us as no time at all. Toward the end of her life (as happens with some of those men and women who have not only learned a discipline inside out, but come to realize how much they still don't know, how much is yet to be discovered), she had about her a real wisdom—not the feigned or pretentious wisdom of yet another late twentieth-century secular guru, but a quiet, humble, wry, though still passionate, interest in the world that got translated, at times, into remarkable observations, which she made unself-consciously, with no eye to who might be ready to venerate and celebrate what had been spoken.

My last visit with her was in late 1980. She would be dead in less than two years, and was already in failing health. I had known her, by then, almost fifteen years, and had much treasured our times together, our correspondence. The latter could be edifying beyond expectation—long letters, sometimes, or brief ones with candid, occasionally brisk and sharp observations, not to mention constant reference to her work as a child psychoanalyst, all delivered in the clearest of narrative prose. During our last meeting (and I knew then it would be fatuous to expect there would be any more) she was quite willing to review some of the past discussions we'd had—about the ways children come to personal terms with those "variables" called "race" and "class," and about the lives of two individuals who meant a lot to me, and about whom I told her a lot: Simone Weil and Dorothy Day.

At one point, as I was talking about those two women, yet again, and more broadly about the way all of us (including children) formulate our religious or spiritual yearnings (or, for that matter, most emphatically formulate a lack of such yearnings), she had this to say: "It comes as no surprise to many parents that a child is for them an opportunity: to discover themselves, their own childhood, once again; to find the only 'immortality' most of us can ever hope to see, in the children we see before us, as I heard a mother once say, 'carrying on, where I'll leave off'—a very tactful way of talking. I am getting around to saying that we can find in children what we are looking for (within limits, yes); and the reason is, we have put there [in them] what we're later so surprised (sometimes) to notice! I'm afraid this [formulation of sorts] applies to us, too [child psychiatrists and psychoanalysts]. We have found in children what we suspected—an endlessly complex psychology. When you started your own work, you found what you suspected: sociology, race, the circumstances in which a family lives—all that has a life in a child's mind. Before any of us [psychoanalysts] appeared on the world scene, others knew what they were looking for: a capacity to *believe*—and they certainly found that capacity in children and learned themselves to work with that capacity! Now, more and more, I hear about biology and the brain, and surely children will help out those [biologically oriented investigators] who are looking at them from that angle!"

She paused long enough to see on my face a mix of consternation and anxiety—as if I were hearing an indictment of all of us who spend time with children: We impose on them, so I feared she was implying, our own agendas—the child as a mirror of us observers, if not an instrument of our ideological passions, maybe even our ambitions. But no, she had something quite else in mind—and she had a way, I'd noted for years, of quietly seeing through someone else's confusions, and without mentioning them, or in any manner putting the person in question on the spot, clarifying her own remarks in such a way that the one she was with, suddenly, was with her, so to speak: "It is natural, all this [that she had described]. What is sad is—when we don't quite realize what we're all doing. Maybe *that* is what my father did for us, after all—give us a way of being more aware of what we do, so we're not so surprised when we finally understand not only what others are doing, but what *we're* doing!"

She was not at all interested in reserving for herself the privileged position of the one who is beyond the limitations and blind spots to which everyone else is heir. Rather, she was reminding herself, never mind me, toward the end of her life, that psychoanalysts (and social scientists, and all sorts of other theory-bent individuals) can single out and explore what is there in the world, but also miss what's there or, alas, dismiss what others notice and regard with great interest as not being worthy of much notice, hence to be put aside with one or another pejorative description: religion as a neurosis, for instance.

During that same meeting, a short one (by our standards) of less than an hour, she came as close to a full and sympathetic interest in spiritual questions as I'd ever heard her manage to do: "The longer you live, the more you realize how little time there is—and how little we really know about this universe! It is impressive—the way some people can put distance between themselves as believers and themselves as human beings, with all the passions we have as human beings. I suppose that is the soul [in them] at work: their ability, at times, to be bigger morally than they usually are. It's a struggle—but they have moral passion, working in the interest of certain ideals. I am not interested in *explaining* those people—only saluting them, some of them, who are such good men and women, and have found for themselves a faith that inspires them. I am not sure there are too many [such people]—I think there are plenty of churchgoers, but maybe far fewer people who really take to heart what those churches were once meant to be!"

Silence, then her signal to me that she was tired: an offer of a refill of coffee. I said I had to go. She said she too "had to go." As I left, I heard myself saying (a free association!): Yes, so do we all, in time, "have to go." As I left, too, I saw, still, her face after she had spoken those last words, made that last observation—a certain wistfulness, an ironic detachment, but also, I thought, a kind of yearning: the great joys of honorable and decent spiritual transcendence (a commitment to the beyond) that some can find, but among them not her.

When Ernest Jones asked Anna Freud what she thought her father's most noteworthy characteristics was, she replied instantly: "his simplicity." He was indeed a man of simple personal habits. He wrote simple prose. He made an astonishing number of observations, and quite simply, quite stubbornly, fought for the intactness of their preservation, so that eventually they would survive over the generations and cross into every continent.

Anna Freud has remained fittingly loyal to her father by refusing to stand in useless awe of his accomplishments. She has gone forward where he left off, giving her life to children from unhappy homes, to children in the midst of the terrors of war, to normal children in their puzzling, inspiring variety. All the while she has written the clear, civilized prose of the confident scientist, the warm, good-humored prose of the kind and sensible human being. The most complicated idea emerges so effortlessly that it seems to be pure "common sense." She has never exploited her name or her profession. She has lived discreetly with her doubts, refusing to allow them to make her strident, pedantic or doctrinaire. She, too, has achieved simplicity.

William Carlos Williams

America obsessed and haunted William Carlos Williams; he could not stop regarding its contradictions and ambiguities, its quite apparent wealth and power, its episodic idealism, its strong appetites—and its mean, self-centered, exploitative side. He never felt satisfied that he had, once and for all, grasped his native country, figured it out and come up with the words that would help others do so. No wonder *Paterson* defies categorization, for all the careful and subtle efforts made by the best intentioned of friends and scholars. Everyone agrees that the poem is a long and ambitious one; but as one tries to estimate exactly where Williams stands and what, finally, he upholds (in the way of doctrine, dogma, faith, or moral beliefs), the imposing turmoil of the poem and the extraordinary stretch of its author's imagination stand in the way. Both the narrator and his subject matter—people, places, things, and not least, the social history of the United States—defy those whom, perhaps, Dr. Williams had in mind as he wrote: the "intellectual heads," as he once called them, who take evidence of inconsistency and confusion as a challenge, requiring yet another theoretical confrontation. The man who is Paterson brims with excitement, vitality, and hopefulness. The man who is Paterson also shows himself to be tired, sad, forlorn and soon enough ready for his last breath. The city that is Paterson grows, surges, and carves out a destiny for itself. The city that is Paterson seems hopelessly doomed almost from the start. Now you see it, now you don't, the poet seems to be saying to his readers; just try and get a "viewpoint" or a "position" out of me (or out of the people I try to evoke, or out of the various situations I address myself to) and you will soon enough be brought up short or left unwittingly high and dry, with a forefinger pointing frantically at but one segment of territory; and such is the fate of those who are or want to be all too sure of themselves.

The child who became William Carlos Williams, poet, novelist, playwright, painter, essayist, inveterate letter-writer, librettist, social historian, and not incidentally, a practicing physician for over half a century, was born to parents whose background was unusual and, no doubt, a source of occasional consternation for a growing boy. His father was English, his mother of Spanish, French, and Jewish ancestry. As if to balance such an inheritance, their son was born and died in Rutherford, New Jersey—these days in America a remarkable fact. But Dr. Williams in certain respects was simply another American; there are elements of fate and social circumstance in his family's past that millions of Americans share, even if they are never destined to live almost eight decades in one state, never mind one town. He had, for example, a grandmother orphaned as a child and desperately poor, who nevertheless made her way across the Atlantic and then up the social ladder, and other relatives scattered in various places outside or inside this country. Williams was not alone when he contemplated the mystery and magic of his existence— that a father and mother of such different origins should even have met.

As a boy he was taken to Europe, even sent to school in Switzerland and France; and as a young man, and later the father of two sons, he was not averse to a return. But he mostly stayed home; more than that, he committed himself resolutely and unstintingly to the life of a small-town doctor. The demands upon him by his patients were constant, heavy, and hard ethically to rebuff—even when outrageous. He could never take even a modest night's sleep for granted; and like all general practitioners (hence their declining number), he had to contend with those explosively irrational moments that patients have in the course of their day-to-day lives. Yet this man who loved New York City and, especially in the 1920s, was drawn to the literary and artistic life of Greenwich Village, never forsook Rutherford—thereby, one can say, facing up to the almost exquisite tensions of his life: all-night vigils beside struggling men, women, and children, followed by a day of office hours and hospital rounds, and in between, a minute here, a minute there, notes to himself for poems, or the actual writing of them.

Even now, nearly a half-century after his death, the exuberant power of Williams's mind touches and persuades those who read his words; he had a contagious vitality and a shaping vision which still beckon. Still, during his lifetime recognition came exceedingly slow. (He was awarded the Pulitzer Prize and the Gold Medal for Poetry posthumously, and he died at almost eighty.) Not that he hadn't taken big risks, thereby offending all sorts of important critics. He once told a young friend that there were moments when he wondered whether much of his dignity didn't rest, finally, on the antagonisms he'd carefully nurtured over the years.

Nevertheless, in the last fifteen or so years of his life, the world of "principalities and powers" began to beckon him. In early 1951, for instance, the Alpha chapter of Phi Beta Kappa at Harvard announced that William Carlos Williams would be the guest poet at its annual commencement meeting in June. He said yes—a particularly significant honor for a writer who had been so constantly suspicious of the academic world. Williams wanted "a local pride," one connected to the industrial working-class city of Paterson, New Jersey, of all places where he practiced medicine so long and hard. At times he was considered and modest in his rejection of a traditionalism and aestheticism that made for (he believed) sterility, pomposity, or self-indulgence. More than occasionally, however, his line of argument became testy and overwrought.

For many weeks he wondered what he ought say in the poem he intended to write for the Harvard occasion. By late March, however, he was an invalid, felled by a serious stroke. By May, miraculously, he was much better and had written his poem, "The Desert Music," which he did indeed deliver, no matter the weakened state of his health.

The poem was a bold and dramatic one. The Cambridge audience was summoned to the Southwest, "between Juarez and El Paso." The subject was the source of human dignity—given the inevitable dark side of our mental and spiritual life, not to mention the social and political tawdriness to be found in all countries. The poet chose a cloistered hall in the Northeast to sing of Texas and Mexico, of forlorn and betrayed Indians, or rowdy, bullying cowboys, of men and women twisted, hurt, debased. Yet his music rescued vitality and humor from the gutter: "What in the form of an old whore in / a cheap Mexican joint in Juarez, her bare / can wiggling crazily can be / so refreshing to me, raise to my ear / so sweet a tune, built of such slime?"

He asked his listeners to think of the whore's "customers," to contemplate how we find our various victims on this earth, how we cultivate a vigorous self-righteousness at the expense of others. Ailing, aware that future strokes were likely, and hence more and more deformity, Williams dared present himself as the old performer, warts and all, struggling, still struggling to find a halfway genuine act—a song and dance that would successfully affirm what he was meant to do: to make the effort, with words, to comprehend life's meaning.

It is ironic that the dean of Harvard Medical School once tried to get Williams to come to talk to a group of doctors at a major medical center. No, the New Jersey loner said; he had nothing to offer, and he was in fact surprised at the mention of any such invitation. For all his spells of urgent egoism (so poignantly and candidly confessed and examined in *Paterson*), William Carlos Williams was in large measure a shy and humble physician whose way with words went relatively unappreciated for a long time indeed. His so-called betters in medicine awed him. Any number of poets and critics awed him—hence his occasional self-protective and accusatory outbursts. We know from his correspondence (and those of us privileged to talk with him remember from his strong-minded words) that Harvard awed him. But he need not have been so self-doubting. Now, his poems, his stories, and his novels command the eager, attentive interest of poets and critics, to be sure, but also of college students and medical students, including those at places such as Harvard.

A great privilege (and actually, turn of fate) befell me in the early 1950s, when I was encouraged by a fine professor-friend of mine, under whose supervision I'd written my undergraduate thesis, to send a note to William Carlos Williams and ask him whether he'd mind reading a college student's effort to understand his poetry, especially the first book of *Paterson*. This inquiry was not thoroughly gratuitous or self-serving, Professor Perry Miller kept insisting—a response to my fearful hesitancy, an attitude which surely (I now realize) protected me from realizing how much of my pride, if not (as today's psychiatrists call it) narcissism had been put into that research and writing effort. This particular poet, Mr. Miller reminded me several times, was hardly a favorite of many college professors, and might well enjoy reading what a student writing in an ivy-covered dormitory library managed to say about *Paterson*, wherein no huge flowering of ivy is recorded.

Soon enough, I'd dispatched my essay, and received a warm, friendly and lively response to it, coupled with an invitation to drop by; and soon enough I did. For me, to know Dr. Williams, to hear him talk about his writing and his life of medical work among the poor and working people of northern New Jersey, was to change direction markedly. Once headed for teaching, I set my sights for medical school. The result was a fairly rough time with both the pre-medical courses, not easy for me, and medical school itself, where I had a lot of trouble figuring out what kind of doctoring I'd be able to do with a modest amount of competence. During those years, ailing though Dr. Williams was, he found the time and energy to give me several much needed boosts—as in this comment: "Look, you're not out on a four-year picnic at that medical school, so stop talking like a disappointed lover. You signed up for a spell of training and they're dishing it out to you, and all you can do is take everything they've got, everything they hand to you, and tell yourself how lucky you are to be on the receiving end—so you can be a doctor, and that's no bad price to pay for the worry, the exhaustion."

Anyone who knew him would recognize the familiar way of putting things, of approaching both another person and this life's hurdles: kind and understanding underneath, but bluntly practical and unsentimental. Not that Williams didn't have in him (and in his writing) a wonderful romanticism, an ardently subjective willingness to take big risks with his mind and heart. His greatest achievement, *Paterson*, is a lyrical examination of a given city's social history, from the early days of this country to the middle of the twentieth century   and the poet whose eyes and ears become the reader's is marvelously vibrant, daring. But there is also in that poem, and in other aspects of Williams's work, a sensible and skeptical voice—the side of Williams his doctor stories reveal to us: a hardworking doctor whose flights of fancy are always being curbed by a sharp awareness of exactly what life demands as well as offers.

I will never forget an exchange I had with Williams when I was in my last year of medical school. He had been sick rather a lot by then, but his feisty spirit was still in evidence, and as well, his canny ability to appraise a situation—anyone or anything—quickly and accurately. I told him I wanted to take a residency in pediatrics. He said "fine," then looked right into my eyes and addressed me this way: "I know you'll like the kids. They'll keep your spirits high. But can you go after them—grab them and hold them down and stick needles in them and be deaf to their noise?" Oh yes, I could do that. Well, he wasn't so sure. Mind you, he wasn't being rudely personal with me. He was just talking as the old man he was, who had seen a lot of patients, and yes, a lot of doctors, too. "Give yourself more time," he urged me, in conclusion. Then he regaled me with some (literally speaking) "doctor stories"—accounts of various colleagues of his: how they did their various jobs; the joys some of them constantly experienced, or alas, the serious troubles a number of them had struggled to overcome; the satisfactions of x, y, z specialties, and conversely, the limitations of those same specialties. It was a discourse, a grand tour of sorts, and I remember to this day the contours of that lively exchange. I told my advisor at medical school about the meeting, and I can still recall those words, too: "You're lucky to know him."

We are all lucky to know him, to have him in our continuing midst. Only in those last years of his life was William Carlos Williams, finally, obtaining the recognition he'd failed to receive for many decades of a brilliantly original, productive literary life. But during that early spell of relative critical neglect (or outright dismissal, or patronizing half-notice) this particular writer could rely upon other sources of approval. Every day of a long medical life (and often enough, in the middle of the night, too) he was called by the men, women and children of northern New Jersey, ordinary people, plain people who considered themselves lucky to hold a job, lucky to be able to get by, barely, or not so lucky, because jobless—families who had one very important loyalty in common, no matter their backgrounds, and they were ethnically diverse: a willingness, an eagerness, a downright determination to consider one Rutherford doctor their doctor, W.C. Williams, M.D. We who think of poets often look wide and far for their spiritual roots, their cultural moorings. William Carlos Williams was one poet who made quite clear who his teachers were, where they lived, how they affected him, helped shape his particular sensibility: "Yet there is/ no return: rolling up out of chaos,/ a nine months' wonder, the city/ the man, an identity—it can't be/ otherwise—an/ interpenetration, both ways."

The city was, of course, Paterson, the Paterson of *Paterson*, the Paterson of industrial strife, of smokestacks and foundries and assembly lines, the Paterson of foreign languages still native tongues, of Italians and Jews and Poles and the Irish and the Blacks, the Paterson of desperately poor people in the 1930s, part of that enormous nation within a nation characterized by Franklin Delano Roosevelt in 1933 as "ill-fed, ill-housed and ill-clothed." As the poet of Paterson declared, he had struggled himself in that city of hard-pressed souls, and so doing, had become very much part of a given human scene—not only the lyric observer or prophet, as in *Paterson* of five epic volumes, but also the obstetrician and gynecologist, the school doctor, the pediatrician, the general practitioner: the young doc and the middle-aged doc and the old doc who drove all over and walked all over and climbed steps all over Paterson (and Rutherford and other New Jersey towns), a family legend to hundreds and hundreds rather than a literary giant (eventually) to hundreds and hundreds of thousands.

"Outside/ outside myself/ there is a world," the poet of *Paterson* declares himself to have "rumbled," and then notes that such a world was "subject" to his "incursions," and was one he made it his business to "approach concretely." No question he did, with all the directness, earthiness, and urgent immediacy of a doctor who knows life itself to be at stake—someone else's, and in a way (professional, moral) his own as well. I remember the doctor describing his work, telling stories that were real events, wondering in retrospect how he did it, kept going at such a pace, hauled himself so many miles a day, got himself up so many stairs, persisted so long and hard with families who had trouble, often enough, using English, never mind paying their bills. And as he knew, and sometimes had to say out loud, even mention in his writing, it wasn't as if he was loaded with money, or a writer who took in big royalties.

America's Depression was a disaster for Dr. Williams's patients, and many of them never paid him much, if indeed, anything at all. America's Depression was also a time when a marvelously versatile, knowing, and gifted writer who happened to be a full-time doctor was not having any great success with critics, especially the powerful ones who claimed for themselves the imprimatur of the academy. No wonder this writing doctor was glad to go "outside" himself, greet and try to comprehend a world other than that of literary people. No wonder, too, he shunned the possibility of a relatively plush Manhattan practice—the doctor to well-known cultural figures. His patients may have been obscure, down and out, even illiterate by the formal testing standards of one or another school system, but they were, he had figured out early on, a splendidly vital people— full of important experiences to tell, memories to recall, ideas to try on their most respected of visitors, the busy doc who yet could be spellbound by what he chanced to hear, and knew to keep in mind at night when the typewriter replaced the stethoscope as his major professional instrument.

I remember asking Williams the usual, dreary question—one I hadn't stopped to realize he'd been asked a million or so times before: how did he do it, manage two full-time careers so well and for so long? His answer was quickly forthcoming, and rendered with remarkable tact and patience, given the provocation: "It's no strain. In fact, the one [medicine] nourishes the other [writing], even if at times I've groaned to the contrary." If he had sometimes complained that he felt drained, overworked, denied the writing time he craved, needed, he would not forget for long all the sustaining, healing, inspiring moments a profession—a calling, maybe, it was in his life—had given him: moment upon moment in the course of more than four decades of medical work.

Such moments are the stuff of Williams's "doctor stories"—the best of their kind since Dr. Anton Chekhov did his (late nineteenth-century) storytelling. As one goes through Williams's evocation of a twentieth-century American medical practice, the sheer daring of the literary effort soon enough comes to mind—the nerve he had to say what he says. These are brief talks, or accounts meant to register disappointment, frustration, confusion, perplexity; or, of course, enchantment, pleasure, excitement, strange or surprising or simple and not at all surprising satisfaction. These are stories that tell of mistakes, of errors of judgment; and as well, of one modest breakthrough, then another—not in research efforts of major clinical projects, but in that most important of all situations, the would-be healer face-to-face with the sufferer who half desires, half dreads the stranger's medical help. As I heard Dr. Williams once say: "Even when the patients knew me well, and trusted me a lot, I could sense their fear, their skepticism. And why not? I could sense my own worries, my own doubts!"

He has the courage to share such raw and usually unacknowledged turmoil with his readers—even as he took after himself in an almost Augustinian kind of self-scrutiny toward the end of the second book of *Paterson*. In almost every story the doctor is challenged not only by his old, familiar antagonist, disease, but that other foe whose continuing power is a given for all of us—pride in all its forms, disguises, assertions. It is this "unreflecting egoism," as George Eliot called it, which the doctor-narrator allows us to see, and so doing, naturally, we are nudged closer to ourselves. Narcissism, as we of this era have learned to call the sin of pride, knows no barriers of race or class—of occupation or profession, either. But as ministers and doctors occasionally realize, there is a sad, inevitable irony at work in their lives—the preacher flawed in precisely the respect he denounces during his sermons, the doctor ailing even as he tries to heal others.

Williams knew the special weakness we all have for those who have a moral hold on us, for those who attend us in our life-and-death times. Williams knew, too, that such a vulnerability prompts gullibility, an abject surrender of one's personal authority—and the result is not only the jeopardy of the parishioner or the patient, but the priest or the physician. Arrogance is the other side of eager acquiescence. Presumptuousness and self-importance are the wounds this life imposes upon those privy to the wounds of others. The busy, capable doctor, well aware of all the burdens he must carry, and not in the least inclined to shirk his duties, may stumble badly in those small moral moments that constantly press upon him or her— the nature of a hello or good-bye, the tone of voice as a question is asked or answered, the private thoughts one has, and the effect they have on our face, our hands as they do their work, our posture, our gait. "There's nothing like a difficult patient to show us ourselves," Williams once said to a medical student, and then he expanded the observation further: "I would learn so much on my rounds, or making home visits. At times I felt like a thief because I heard words, lines, saw people and places—and used it all in my writing. I guess I've told people that, and no one's so surprised! There was something deeper going on, though—the *force* of all those encounters. I was put off guard again and again, and the result was—well, a descent into myself."

He laughed as he said that, and worried about a comparison he nevertheless proceeded to make—with the achievement of "insight" in psychoanalysis. I say "worried" because he knew rather well that he had in mind a moral as well as psychological or emotional confrontation, and he'd been hearing a lot in those last years of his life (to his amazement and chagrin) about a supposedly "value-free" psychoanalysis or social science. Not that he couldn't put aside his anger and disgust and simply laugh at his own pretensions and spells of blindness, at those of others. His stories abound with such self-mocking gestures—parody turned on the parodist, words used to take the stern (but also compassionate) measure of the doctor who dispensed (among other things) words, and then went home to dish them out—well, "in the American grain." It is important to emphasize the humorous and tolerant side of this storytelling self-arraignment of a singular New Jersey doctor: even the terribly hurt, driven, melancholy "Old Doc Rivers" is not without his spirited decency—a dizzying mix of selfless honor, passionate concern, and alas, the unrestrained demonic constantly at work.

These stories are, really, frank confidences extended to the rest of us by one especially knowing, dedicated physician who was willing to use his magical gifts of storytelling in a gesture of—what? We all require forgiveness, and we all hope to redeem our own missteps—hope, through whatever grace is granted us, to make every possible reparation. Words were the instrument of grace given to this one doctor, and words are the instrument of grace, also, for the rest of us, the readers who have and will come upon these marvelously provocative tales. As Dr. Williams's beloved wife Flossie (she appears now and then in his medical fictions) once said to me: "There's little in a doctor's life Bill didn't get at when he wrote." She'd been there with him, of course, all along, and she knew: the periods of irritability and impatience; the flashes of annoyance and resentment; the instance of greed, or just plain bitterness that "they" can't, don't, won't pay up; the surge of affection—even desire, lust; the assertion of power—a fierce wish to control, to tell in no uncertain terms, to win at all costs; the tiredness, the exhaustion, the despondency. The rush of it all, the fast-paced struggle, again and again, with all sorts of illnesses—and the victories over them, the defeats at their hands, and not least, the realization (postmortem) of one's limitations, one's mistakes.

For years I taught Williams's doctor stories to medical students, and during each class we all seemed newly awakened—encouraged to ask the important whys, consider the perplexing ifs. The stories offer medical students and their teachers an opportunity to discuss the big things, so to speak, of the physician's life—the great unmentionables that are, yet, everyday aspects of doctoring: the prejudices we feel (and feel ashamed of), the moments of spite or malice we try to overlook, the ever loaded question of money, a matter few of us like to discuss, yet one constantly stirring us to pleasure, to bedeviling disappointment in others, in ourselves. What, in fact, that is really important has Williams left out? Nothing, it seems. He gives us a chance to discuss the alcoholic doctor, the suicidal doctor. He prompts us to examine our ambitions, our motives, our aspirations, our purposes, our worrying lapses, our grave errors, our overall worth. He gives us permission to bare our souls, to be candidly introspective, but not least, to smile at ourselves, to be grateful for the continuing opportunity we have to make recompense for our failures of omission or commission.

He extends to us, really, moments of a doctor's self-recognition—rendered in such a way that the particular becomes the universal, and the instantly recognizable: the function, the great advantage of all first-rate art. And not to be forgotten in this age of glib, overwrought formulations, of theories and more theories, of conceptualizations meant to explain (and explain away) anything and everything, he brings to us ironies, paradoxes, inconsistencies, contradictions—the small vignette which opens up a world of pleasurable, startling, or forbidden mystery. Doc Williams becomes William Carlos Williams the accomplished fabulist, anecdotist—and as well, the medical and social historian who takes the risks of autobiography. There were poems similarly harnessed, intended, and even journal entries, as in this wonderful statement found in the "little red notebook" Williams the Rutherford School Physician kept in 1914:

I bless the muscles
of their legs, their
necks that are
limber, their hair
that is like new
grass, their eyes
that are not
always dancing
their postures
so naive and
graceful, their
voices that are
full of fright &
other passions
their transparent
shams & their

mimicry of adults
—the softness of
their bodies—

As I read through, once more, Williams's medical stories, medical poems, and the autobiographical account, "The Practice," all so touching and blunt, both, I kept returning to the words just quoted, to which I'd once heard him allude, and which I remember him trying to remember, to speak—the powerful, compelling, sensuousness of his mind, with its offering of a hymn of love to those children, those patients, those fellow human beings. On a few occasions physicians invited him to come speak at their conferences, their grand rounds, but he was shy, modest—afraid he had little to say directly to his colleagues, no matter how much he'd offered the world in general through his many and varied writings. But he was dead wrong; he had everything to say to us. He opens up the whole world, our world, to us—and so, once again, as many in New Jersey had occasion to say, say and say again: thank you, Doctor Williams.

Walker Percy

Walker Percy is now best known as a novelist, and deservedly
so. *The Moviegoer*, *The Last Gentleman*, *Love in the Ruins*,
and *Lancelot* have earned him substantial but limited recognition;
substantial because he has been given critical praise and obtained
a loyal following, but limited because by no means has he become a
well-known American writer, and some of his most avid readers still
think of him as the property of a relative handful—no underground
writer, and no member of a small coterie, yet someone not known
in the way Saul Bellow or John Updike or Robert Penn Warren is
known. Some who are familiar with his writing regard him as more
than a novelist and essayist: as, rather, a philosopher, a man of special
understanding and humor, a person who helps the reader think altogether differently about life, a person, too, through whom one can
recognize spiritual comrades—namely those who also have found
their lives strongly affected by Walker Percy's articles and books.

I may well be describing myself. I have no distance, certainly,
on Dr. Percy's writing; I have liked it intensely and consistently for
many years. I remember reading his articles during the 1950s, when
I was learning to be a doctor, then a psychiatrist. I especially remember coming across "The Man on the Train," which appeared
in *Partisan Review*. The year was 1956, and the article was recom-

mended to a few of us stray souls who had ventured from academic libraries, or, in my case, a hospital clinic, to a seminar on systematic theology taught by Paul Tillich at Harvard. I can still hear Tillich saying emphatically, as we were leaving the classroom one day: "Percy is a physician, I believe." I would have read anything Tillich recommended, no mind if the suggested author were a garbage collector, a madman, a theoretical physicist. For me at that time Tillich offered surcease, to use a somewhat out-of-fashion word *he* occasionally used—a relief from dogmatic, presumptuous, and all too self-confident psychiatric generalizations. If some supervisors encouraged narrow reductionism, Tillich was there at Harvard, two afternoons a week, full of passion and ready to insist upon the mystery of things, the strange and fateful "moments," he often called them, that make such a difference in our lives. The reading of "The Man on the Train" turned out to be such a moment in my life. The article was intended to bring readers up short, to prompt in them a thought or two about why they were doing what, day in and day out. It was a philosophical essay; it took up, yet again, the old Socratic question of "life's meaning," but did so in a lively, humorous way—offering psychological and sociological observations almost casually, as if they were important, yes, but had to be taken with a few grains of salt. It was a little harder, after reading the essay several times, and hearing Paul Tillich talk about it, to be quite so self-important, quite so sure of oneself and one's various ideas—or, in the clinic, one's "interpretations."

The fateful "mystery of things" that Tillich kept mentioning soon had me encountering Dr. Percy's first published novel, *The Moviegoer*, under somewhat unusual circumstances. I was living in Biloxi, Mississippi—stationed there, at Keesler Air Force Base, as an air force captain, in charge of a neurological and psychiatric unit at the military hospital. I was also going to nearby New Orleans almost every late afternoon in order to attend medical and psychiatric conferences and pursue psychoanalytic training. Each weekday I drove through Gentilly, where Binx Bolling of *The Moviegoer* lived. Since

I was in psychoanalysis at the time, I was perhaps given to more ruminations than usual—efforts to figure out not only how I had come to be the kind of person I was, but what I ought do with my life, and, not least, what "meaning" there is in that more generic use of the word *life*.

The movies: I'd been going to them more and more—so much that I couldn't find enough to see for the first time on any given day. (This was not New York, or Cambridge, where in fact I'd not gone much at all, but "La.-Miss.," as the combined two-state abbreviation was often rendered on advertisements.) I'd go to see my analyst every afternoon, and I'd go to a movie afterwards, then there'd be a girlfriend, a long ride in the car, a jazz bar—and, too commonly, memories of the movie intruding in my mind as I talked with the young lady, or as I made hospital rounds the next morning and talked with all those tough, strong, brave SAC pilots who were defending us against anyone and everyone and flying incredible speeds in incredible planes—and were also breaking down in fear and in tears, unaccountably it always seemed.

"Doc, what in hell does this life mean?" one hotshot jet pilot kept asking me, and some scene out of some movie would come to mind—*Purple Noon*, for example, which I saw five times, and wherein the hero (Alain Delon) gets away with everything (money, love, adventure) and sails into the warm, Mediterranean sun: *that's* the meaning of life!

"Why do you keep seeing *Purple Noon*?" my Prytania Street doctor asked. "Why do you see those James Dean movies over and over—what do they, what does he, *mean* to you?"

"Dunno." Then, on my back, my face turned toward the wall, I would see a scene in *East of Eden* or *Rebel without a Cause*, or one or another John Wayne movie, or Billy Holden in *Sunset Boulevard*, a movie I'd not seen when it came out (1950, I believe) but saw three times in three days in New Orleans in 1960.

The Moviegoer was published on May 15, 1961. I read it in the fall
of that year—an obscure novel, headed for extinction, a few hundred copies sold, mostly in New Orleans.

"He lives here, in Covington, across the Lake" (Pontchartrain)
I was told by the clerk in Doubleday's bookstore on Canal Street,
when I seemed to be clutching at the book, afraid to let it go, so he
could (all he wanted!) see the price.

I missed my movie that afternoon and evening. I phoned "a certain someone," as the author of *The Moviegoer* puts it, to claim illness. I finished the novel around midnight. I took a slug or two of
bourbon: who *is* this Walker Percy?

"But the real question," said the Prytania Street analyst the next
day, "is who are you?"

"What do you mean?"

"You're always asking questions in response to my questions."

"What do you mean?"

"There you go again."

"Well, I'm now seeing that movie *Purple Noon* again—the sky,
the water, the boat speeding away."

"You are?"

"Yes." Long silence.

For me Walker Percy's writing has offered a continuing intensity of
awareness and, I suppose, self-recognition. His writing has made
me feel less lonely and more in touch with this world: his has been a
voice in the wilderness, to use a phrase, and a voice that makes one's
own high-pitched raspy drone seem less peculiar and, yes, not quite
so loony. To my mind Binx was, for all too long I fear, myself writ
large—put into a book, rendered for others.

"You seem to be shadowing Binx," the New Orleans doctor said.

I was making a decision about my life during 1960, when *The Moviegoer* appeared; I decided to stay South, to live in New Orleans upon

discharge from the air force, so that I could work with the four small
black children who were then getting ready to initiate school desegregation (against persistent and violent resistance, as it turned out).
I have, in the first volume of *Children of Crisis*, described how I came
to that decision, after witnessing a "swim in" by blacks on a Biloxi
beach, and seeing them almost killed. It was a decision that would
change my life. For almost two decades I have been trying to get to
know children in various parts of this country who are struggling
against various social, economic, racial odds, children who manage
to survive—and who sometimes show extraordinary courage rather
than the various "symptoms" one like me is trained to spot and try
to "treat." Walker Percy's novel gave hope to me, helped me feel
stronger at a critical time, when I was somewhat lost, confused, vulnerable, and, it seemed, drifting badly. The "hope" I mention, the
"stronger" sense of conviction, were personal responses to a writer
whose essays I had been following, whose novel struck home with
such force that I felt less bewildered and distracted than I had in a
long time—and, in Heidegger's sense of the expression, more "at
home" with myself.

I read *The Moviegoer* over and over again; I would be embarrassed
to list the number of times. To be honest, I lost count. On each reading I discovered something new that was amusing or instructive—or
provided yet another reason to return to Sören Kierkegaard, Martin Heidegger, and Gabriel Marcel, to whom (all three) I had been
introduced first by Perry Miller, as an undergraduate, and then by
Paul Tillich in the seminar of his I took while studying psychiatry.
And then, there were the children I was getting to know in New Orleans, white and black; they, too, had good reason to stop and think
about things, to question "life" in the way a severe crisis can prompt
some of us to do. Here is an eight-year-old child, born and reared in
that city, wondering (the year was 1962) about "things," after a long
and painful stretch of months in a classroom completely boycotted
by white boys and girls: "I will ask myself if it's worth it. I will ask
myself why God made people like He did those white people who

shout all those bad words at me. I will ask myself if it makes any sense, to keep walking by them, and trying to smile at them, and trying to be polite, when I'd like to see them all dead. I would! But the minister says we are tested—that's why we're put here in the world, to be tested. So, I guess I ought to thank those white folks. They're testing me!

"I try to talk to God when I walk past them. I ask Him please to help me do what is right—to know what I should do. It's not easy, knowing what to do. I'll bet you can find some people who have grown old, and they still aren't sure how you're supposed to live your life. They're still wondering what's it all about! My grandfather is one of those people! That's what he always asks: 'What's it all about?' He takes his whiskey when he comes home from his job, and he sits on the porch, on his rocking chair—he built it himself, and you can pull it apart and store it, and then put it back together, real easy. While he's sitting, and he's sipping, he does his asking. He asks God a lot of questions, and he asks my momma and my poppa, and he asks himself, and he'll even ask me.

"The other day, he said to me: 'Little one, why do you do like you do?' I knew what he was asking. I told him that I'd heard the Sunday School teacher tell us that we're here to do the best we can to be good, and to show God that He was right when He gave us our freedom—to be good, or to be bad. I try to be good. When those white people tell me they'll kill me, I bite my lip. I don't answer them back the way they talk to me. I try to pray for them. I don't really want to; but I do. I wonder, sometimes, if they ever stop and ask themselves why they are put here in this world. If we don't ask why we're here, we're lost in the woods. That's what I believe. My daddy says so. My granddaddy says so."

None of Walker Percy's novels features a child like her, but his main characters are haunted by the same vexing, puzzling matters she kept coming back to all the time. A dangerous social and racial struggle became for that girl not only an educational opportunity, and a decisive psychological experience, but an occasion for philosophical speculation. More than an occasion; she continued to ask herself important ethical and religious questions as she grew up. She took philosophy courses, read Dostoevski and Tolstoy, Kafka and Camus in college—and yes, the novels of Walker Percy. Somehow, in my mind, her experiences (both subjective and objective), which it was my job to try to comprehend, become linked with Walker Percy and his writing. They lived not all that far away—she on the eastern outskirts of New Orleans, near Gentilly, and he north of the city, across Lake Pontchartrain. They are both Southerners, both of their families originally from Mississippi. They have both known, perhaps, a little more anguish or despair than many others, and have both been prompted, accordingly, to look within themselves and around at others—in order to get their bearings and keep them, not only for the long haul (as in "a philosophy of life") but day after day.

And I guess I have myself shared some of their concerns. One can't spend years with children like that girl, or, indeed, the same years reading Walker Percy, without finding more and more time for some of the questions characters like Binx Bolling, Will Barrett, and Tom More ask, or Percy himself asks in various articles, or, again, a number of children ask, if given a chance to talk about themselves at any length. Much of the work I have been doing since the late 1950s, represented by the five volumes of *Children of Crisis*, has been devoted to the evocation for others of the introspective thoughts, philosophical speculations, and ethical concerns I have heard a number of different American children express during various conversations. I have relied upon Dr. Percy's ideas constantly in the course of that work—to the point that I can scarcely imagine how I would have thought about either my own life or the lives of the children, parents, teachers I have met, were he to have decided, long ago, to keep his important and instructive thoughts to himself, deny them the access to others that essays offer in one way, the novel offers in another.

Especially the last two volumes of *Children of Crisis* connect with

Percy's writing. Indians and Eskimos have no hesitation to look
with open eyes and quizzically at the world—to ask rather rou-
tinely the most important of questions, the most uninhibited and
far-reaching *why*'s; and as for our well-to-do children, they have
often gone through some of the hurdles the author of *The Moviegoer,*
The Last Gentleman, Love in the Ruins, and *Lancelot* has his various
characters try to get through in such a way that they do more than
shrug and grasp the next "deal." In one "country day school" north
of Boston that I visited for several years a teacher told me that some
of her children ("even the young ones, of nine or ten") ask questions
which struck her as "existential." What did she mean?

One asks her, of course—and gets a considered reply: "They have
everything, these children—except a knowledge or conviction of
what to live by. No one teaches them that here. They don't go to
church anymore—and even if they did, all they'd be hearing about
is the value of a 'community,' or of 'mental health.' And at home
it's golf and tennis, skiing or swimming, cocktails and dinner, the
theatre or a trip—until you hear the parents saying that they can't
figure out where all the years have gone, but now the kids are grown
up. And when those kids are grown up they're ready to go on the
same merry-go-round. But when they're ten or twelve, they have a
question or two on their minds. I try to answer those questions. I try
to talk with children who want to know—even if it's just for a few
seconds—what life is all about. That's the way they often put it to
me: 'What is life all about?' I tell them I don't know. I ask them to
get more specific. I say pick one part of life, and maybe we can talk.
Sometimes they do."

So it goes, research, or the search: a teacher who herself has been
a fan of Walker Percy's talks to a doctor who is interested in some
of the same issues Percy keeps examining; they talk about children
no less inclined to ask the same pointed, even haunting, questions
Heidegger, Marcel, and Percy have posed for us in this century.
Through conversations with teachers like her and children she mentions I have been enabled to understand Walker Percy in the way

he, perhaps, would find desirable: ideas exchanged amid a growing willingness to take risks—a step or two, while talking, in the direction of a shared trust. Certainly Walker Percy has taken risks—when he writes and, just as important, in the way he has tried to spend his time on this earth. Not that he has a taste for the dramatic, the irregular, the unconventional. He is, if anything, modest, retiring, a bit shy even, though quite approachable and affable. He is, in one sense, just another resident of Covington, Louisiana. But he has lived his very own life. A doctor, he has never practiced medicine. He has written with obvious understanding about psychiatry and psychoanalysis—to the point that he or those who publish his essays must upon occasion remind readers that he is not a psychiatrist. In fact, through both his articles and his novels he has contributed a good deal to a much needed but still incomplete social history of the feverish involvement between America's agnostic, secularist bourgeoisie and Freud's thinking. Kate in *The Moviegoer* is seeing a psychiatrist. Will Barrett of *The Last Gentleman* has put in his time with one. *Love in the Ruins*, with its main character a doctor, has page after page of sharp observations on alienists (as they used to be called in the nineteenth century—and how ironic, that word, for those who have followed the twentieth-century existentialist literature of "alienation"). In *Lancelot*, the main character is seriously troubled, is in a hospital for the criminally insane, where (the length of the novel) he talks to a psychiatrist who is also a priest.

Percy himself has been "alienated"—from the alienated ones upon whom he has for so long kept his intent eyes. He is a loner. He belongs to no "school" of writers. He is the darling of no literary clique. As a child he lost his parents, went to live with an extraordinary relative, William Alexander Percy, himself a loner, a writer who happened to have a profession (the law). After medical school, Walker Percy spent many months in a sanitarium, virtually alone, recovering from tuberculosis—and, no doubt, from the death of his beloved "Uncle Will," which took place in 1942. There is, surely, a connection between Walker Percy's life and the ideas of those philosophers and novelists who have meant so much to him. They were all "a pretty strange bunch," he once said to me, and he did not, I think, thereby mean to establish any great psychological distance for himself. He has been relatively well-to-do, has not had to hold a job, day after day. He hasn't, that is, been compelled to make the adjustments and accommodations most people find to be a necessary part of everyday life: fit into a "work-team," fit into an "office situation," fit into the demands of a particular institution. He might have become increasingly aloof, removed in spirit as well as substance from the rest of his countrymen, who know and submit to dozens of social, economic, and psychological imperatives he has never had to experience. Yet he has tried hard to stay in touch with others; and maybe, ironically, has been enabled by his own situation to understand how the rest of us manage better than it is possible for us ourselves to do.

He immersed himself for years in the European, Christian, and secular existentialist tradition of both the nineteenth and twentieth centuries—a tradition with its fair share of intent, and intense outsiders. But in his articles, and especially in his novels, he brought that tradition across the Atlantic to the United States of America. His has been an effort to show American readers how the abstract speculations of Heidegger, the more passionate or lyrical speculations of Marcel, have a bearing on daily life in any town of any of our fifty states. And similarly with Kierkegaard or Dostoevski. And Sartre and Camus. But, as an American, Percy has not only attempted translation or evocation; he has balanced a contemporary Christian existentialism with the pragmatism and empiricism of an American physician.

The "search" of my book's title (*Walker Percy: An American Search*) still goes on. I began to write a part of that book as a long profile for *The New Yorker*. I wrote another part for presentation at Yale, as the Trumbull Lectures of 1976. But I had been taking notes on Percy's writing for some time, and writing to myself "messages" or "communications" (to use two of his favorite words) for many years.

I regard him as a pilgrim; the essays that have been collected (1975) into *The Message in the Bottle* are the notes of a man in search of life's meaning—what in another age was called "God's gracious presence." I connect Dr. Percy, maybe out of my own peculiar inclinations, with another Southerner, Flannery O'Connor, and with two French writers, Simone Weil and Georges Bernanos—four Catholic travelers of serious purpose indeed. I hope one day, God willing, to spell out some of those connections; they keep coming to my mind as I keep thinking about those four, the life and writing of each of whom has meant so much to me. Meanwhile, my writing about Percy is a mixture: biography; literary analysis; and, I hope, a "response" in Gabriel Marcel's sense of the word—an act of "fidelity," he might say—to a writer, by an admiring reader.

※※※

For me, writing about Percy's work was a way of learning what I believed—how I saw and comprehended this world. I had, long ago it now seems, "shadowed Binx," as many of us have—lucky and comfortable heirs of Western civilization who nevertheless are quizzical, at loose ends often enough, and not sure what really matters, even as we go about our appointed rounds, accumulating certifications and cash and nods and having our "relationships." Now older, I see Binx still, in my students and my patients, in my sons growing up, and still in myself as I catch myself up to his (my) old tricks; and I think of Binx while walking and noticing, driving and forgetting, stopping and all of a sudden—yes, feeling that one, by god, *is*: that elusive *being* of those high-and-mighty existential philosophers. In a sense, then, doing a certain kind of biography of Percy has in this instance meant not so much dealing with this or that challenge, so far as the subject goes, as coming to terms with one's subjectivity.

To repeat the old question: who is this Walker Percy? He is, a biographer finds out, not only a doctor, an essayist, a novelist, but a rather thoughtful and humorous and unpretentious human being. I think of him, again, as a friend, a person of wisdom—with whom to correspond, to whom one turns for a now-and-then conversation or a drink or two of bourbon. Is friendship fair game as a variable, to be discussed as an aspect of the relationship that develops between biographer and subject? Is a "good and decent example" another variable? Ought we mention the pleasure we've obtained—the fortunate and delightful encounter with a wry, quiet, but strong and lively intelligence? We are all (in one or another way or moment) lonely, as those existentialists Walker Percy knows so well have insisted again and again. Still, their own tradition is sturdy and growing and, not least, a real and mighty help to us. Each of them is a presence for many of us (and a book can be a persuasive companion), and so we may often feel less lonely. Sometimes I will look at my Percy shelf and think of statements I've heard him make, of time spent chewing the fat with him (and dissolving it in a good, strong amber fluid), and incline, just then at least, a little more toward *yes* in respect to this life rather than toward *no* or *maybe*; a consequence, for one soul, not of "doing work on" or "doing a biography of" but *getting to know* another soul.

Dorothy Day

Ifirst met Dorothy Day at a distance. In the 1950s I was a medical student, and much interested in getting away from the cloister of a decidedly academic experience in which patients were unfortunately becoming for me just a bundle of signs and symptoms. I was also struggling hard to connect a strong interest in moral philosophy to the work I was learning as a member of a particular profession—one supposedly close in its everyday preoccupations to what used to be called "ultimate concerns," many of which, alas, seem to be ardently pursued these days in courses called "psychological counseling" or "interviewing techniques." A visit to a Catholic Worker "hospitality house," located in one of New York City's poorer districts, helped me enormously—bridged, a bit, an abstract interest with a concrete situation. There Dorothy Day was, freely acknowledging without embarrassment her own reasons for feeding and clothing the extremely needy—"the lame, the halt, the blind," as she often put it, thereby demonstrating a preference for a biblical rather than sociological language.

Eventually I came to know her; know her great kindness and her constant example of religious faith; know her almost uncanny mix of selfless devotion to the humble ones with wry detachment—as if her soul was in closest communion across time and space with

60

Dostoyevski and Tolstoy, those two nineteenth-century Russian fellow Christians who meant so much to her, and whose books, I think it fair to say without the slightest exaggeration, haunted her every day of her life. One day, she permitted me to scribble some notes as she talked; another time, I took with me a tape recorder, virtually a venerated instrument of a pagan faith (social science). I was bothering her with my confusions and curiosities, much of them centered on what I took to be her "inconsistency"—a radical political life, a conservative religious one. She wanted no part of the distinction: "I don't act politically on the street or worship in church in order to fit in with people who are 'radical,' or people who are 'conservative.' I read the Bible. I try to pay attention to the life of Jesus Christ, our Lord. I try to follow His example. I stumble all the time, but I try to keep going—along the road He walked for us. I am a Catholic, of course; I belong to a Church, and when I made the decision to join it, I knew my whole life would change. For me, everything is religious—politics and the family and work, they all are part of our obligation: to follow our Lord's way."

She was, as she herself put it, "a fool for Christ." She was an utterly devout Catholic who, with Bernanos and Mauriac, knew that the Church today will falter, will fail in its mission, will become badly flawed—and yet, is a chosen instrument of His. Even as Judas once betrayed Him, the clergy now do, and parishioners now do—man's sinful nature. Still, there is hope—and Dorothy Day knew where to look for it: not in the pagan state; not in the dreary banalities and faddish abstractions of social science; not in the cultivation of self; not in a rampant, crazy consumerism; but in the daily struggle to obey God and live a life that does as much justice as possible to His constantly demonstrated lovingkindness. "All the way to Heaven is Heaven," she observed, again and again, quoting Catherine of Siena, who added, "because He said, 'I am the Way.'" Her life, then, gave us a glimpse of Heaven—we who have to live with the knowledge that Hell has a far larger claim on our journey than on that of Dorothy Day.

The family background of Dorothy Day was solid, patriotic, and middle class. Her father's family was of Scotch-Irish ancestry, based in Tennessee: they had fought in the Civil War on the Confederate side. Her mother's family was of English ancestry; from upstate New York, they had fought on the Union side. Her parents were married in an Episcopal church on Perry Street in Greenwich Village, where their daughter would spend many years. John Day was a journalist, a racetrack enthusiast, and eventually one of the founders of Hialeah, the first racetrack in Florida. For a time he wrote a column for the New York *Morning Telegraph*, "On and Off the Turf." At the time of his death he was a member of the New York State commission that kept a watch on racetrack activities. Her mother, born Grace Satterlee, cared for the children, encouraged them, and told them what mattered and what did not.

John and Grace Day's third child and first daughter, Dorothy, was born on November 8, 1897, in New York City. Her two older brothers, Donald and Sam Houston, would both become respectable, conservative journalists—Sam, eventually, managing editor of the New York *Journal American*. Dorothy's only sister, Della, to whom she was strongly attached, was two years her junior. The family moved from New York City to San Francisco in 1904, when Dorothy was seven years old. The 1906 San Francisco earthquake destroyed many buildings, among them one where John Day worked as a sports writer. The Day family soon left for Chicago, where they settled on Chicago's South Side. Because Dorothy's father could not find employment easily, he ended up trying to write a novel, which was never published. In 1907, however, he got a job as the sports editor of *The Inter Ocean*, a Chicago paper, and the family was able to move to the North Side of the city.

When she was sixteen, Dorothy entered the University of Illinois in Urbana, where she would stay only two years. While there she began to call herself a Socialist and to establish friendships with others who, on that midwestern campus, dared pick up the threads of American populism, which had been so influential several decades earlier in the South and the prairie states. At college she was an average student. To supplement her scholarship grant, which she won in a competition supported by the Hearst newspaper the Chicago *Examiner*, she worked at the local Y, changing linen at the dining room tables, and she did household work for professors. At this time she also began to dream of becoming a journalist, a writer. She met a fellow student, Rayna Simons, the daughter of a wealthy Jewish business family. Soon both Dorothy and Rayna became caught up in socialist hopes and concerns. These two students, who became good friends and shared a room, were to live strikingly dramatic and unusual lives. Rayna became a Communist and went to China, then Russia. Her life story—her political and moral pilgrimage—was told in Vincent Sheean's *Personal History*. He desperately wanted to marry her, but she refused him, though she was obviously drawn to him. She died in Moscow of encephalitis in 1927, a little more than a decade after she and Dorothy Day met.

By the time she was nineteen, Dorothy Day had left college and was living in New York, working as a reporter for *The Call*, a socialist paper. Her career as a journalist had started and would continue for the rest of her life. In her early twenties she became very much a part of the radical Greenwich Village scene. Her interest and involvement were based less on theory and ideology than on observation of the world around her and a passionate sense of justice. Her writings were those of a pamphleteer aroused by the poverty and suffering that persisted during America's post–World War I "return to normalcy." She was especially drawn to those who were trying to change the country—labor organizations and people on picket lines. She did not, however, turn her back on the brilliance of the New York intellectual scene. Through her involvement with *The Masses*, she came to know such writers as Mike Gold, Max Eastman, and Floyd Dell, as well as John Dos Passos and Malcolm Cowley. For a while, living on MacDougal Street in Greenwich Village, she seemed to be in continuous conversation—going to lunches and suppers and meetings, waking up with ideas to share with others, and falling asleep with ideas she could barely wait to offer. In 1917, only twenty, she was already in a Washington, D.C., jail, having marched with the suffragettes.

On her return to New York City, she was somewhat aimless. She had left *The Call* and for a while thought she wanted to be a nurse. She took training at Kings County Hospital in Brooklyn for a year but dropped out, unable to sustain the necessary discipline. She worked on the *Liberator*, a radical magazine. She spent a lot of time at the Provincetown Playhouse and had long talks, there and elsewhere, with Eugene O'Neill. They became very close and were known as companions, though the extent of their relationship remains unclear. She also became involved in an unhappy love affair with a tough ex-newspaperman named Lionel Moise, became pregnant by him, had an abortion, and soon thereafter, on the rebound, married Barkeley Tobey, a strange man about whom little is known beyond gossip and the fact that he married eight times. They went to Europe in 1920 and stayed there for a year; Day has made reference to her heavy drinking at that time. When they came back to the States they separated permanently.

Day decided to go to Chicago, where she immediately sought the company of her old midwestern friends, whose populist critique of America's 1920s conservatism had not abated at all. There she went to jail once more, picked up as "dangerous" with her IWW (International Workers of the World, known as "Wobblies") fellow activists during the "red raids" of the period. She spent only a few days in jail, but she would always have a strong memory of that particular experience—the feeling of confinement, of course, but also the degradation of the jailers as well as the jailed. She was touched, too, by the sight of other inmates, the poor, sad people incarcerated for petty crimes and misdemeanors, who, whether they were guilty or not guilty, were clearly headed nowhere. The sentimental side of her, never weak, may well have tried to ignore the specific wrongdoings of those people. Her account of her stay in jail dwells mainly on the prostitutes with whom she shared a cell, particularly their stubborn determination and their generosity and kindness to her.

She would often hark back to that prison stay in the conversations I had with her. Once she told me that "the experience of being in jail *then* [after the turmoil she had been through in her emotional life] had a strong impact" on her way of looking at the world. She came to prison a Wobbly in spirit, full of egalitarian dreams for America. She left prison in a less romantic frame of mind with concrete memories of women who could be called streetwalkers, prostitutes, whores, and names that would call attention to their law-breaking lives, but whose fate kept pushing her to moral reflection. She was, by that time, quite ready to accept the paradox of kindly, sensitive women who helped her get through the days in prison yet could go back on the street to sell themselves, perhaps to steal, and be cruelly indifferent to others in the course of their everyday lives.

Often, as I talked with her, I felt her discomfort with certain memories—discomfort, really, with her earlier life and her "bohemian" past. She seemed uncomfortable even with the aspects of her past that persisted as strengths in her later life: the writer, the political activist, the woman prepared to break ranks with society's norms in order to uphold moral principles. Several times she told me that her "life really did begin" when she "met Peter [Maurin]," and she grew annoyed when I demurred. Yet the continuities in her life are striking; in her "fast" life of the early 1920s and the life that followed her conversion to Catholicism, the same awareness and ideals can be found.

For example, when she thought back to the Wobbly incident and her jailing, she would talk of a particular inmate, Mary-Ann, who was especially considerate and made that stay behind bars much more bearable. A woman who had little education, she was "a woman of the streets," but also a teacher, not unlike Peter Maurin, both in her message, as Dorothy Day recalled it, and in her influence on the person whose life supposedly "began" only years later.

"I can still hear Mary-Ann giving me my lessons in survival—how to get along with the people running the prison," she once told me. Then she spelled out Mary-Ann's teaching—a mix of ethical exhortation and practicality: " 'You must hold up your head high, and give them no clue that you're afraid of them or ready to beg them for anything, any favors whatsoever. But you must see them for what they are—never forget that they're in jail, too.' " A pause, then: "Many times, so many times, I remember that admonition. Mary-Ann had no use for organized religion. She had never finished high school, but in her head and her heart she had somehow drawn near our Lord. Nearer than I was able to get, then. Who knows, nearer than some of us ever get."

During that prison stay Dorothy Day read the Bible, taking particular comfort in the Psalms. But she was not yet tempted by "organized religion." In Chicago she continued her journalistic endeavors and investigated the way the courts treated juveniles and prostitutes. Ben Hecht and Charles MacArthur, who were her friends, were doing similar muckraking. She also worked a while as a clerk in a library, a proofreader, a restaurant cashier, and a clerk in a Montgomery Ward's. She even posed for art classes. The word *drifting* has been applied to this time of her life. Yet one gathers from listening to her that while going from job to job to eke out a living, she was trying to learn how all sorts of people spend their working lives. She wasn't simply "slumming." She had been on her own since she left home for college at seventeen. Her father and older brothers had never approved of her manner of living, her political sympathies, or her activism. Moreover, in the 1920s it was not easy for a woman, especially one who was thoughtful about social and economic matters and critical of America's politics, to find a decent job. For a while she tried New Orleans, where she worked with the *Item*, lived in the French Quarter, and, as a journalist, returned to her interest in exploited women. "I wrote articles on dance-hall girls," she once put it, and yet again, as she talked about them, one could hear her empathy for what such women experience and a willingness—perhaps in the tradition of her friend "Gene" O'Neill—to see them as judges of the rest of us, rather than as morally flawed or suspect.

While in Chicago she had written an autobiographical novel, *The Eleventh Virgin*. Years later she would regret ever having published it and wished that every extant copy could through some magic be destroyed. In New Orleans she learned that Hollywood had bought the book for $5,000, a substantial sum at the time. The novel is candid about the young heroine—her lusty and unconventional life, her brief and tragic romance, her abortion, her loveless marriage, and her constant traveling. The wretched plot is lightened by the narrator's sense of humor and her capacity to observe ordinary people, the strangers we all see but tend not to notice. Whether she was in jail, simply walking in the street, buying groceries, asking directions, browsing in a bookstore, or waiting in line to enter a theater or a museum, Dorothy Day was constantly noticing people, constantly ready to engage with them and let them become, even for a few moments, part of her life. This unusual quality, which I watched at work in her, would not yield even to old age, a time when so many of us are inclined to put more and more barriers between ourselves and others, often impelled to do so by nature itself: the way aging can isolate us, restricting both our mental and physical capacities.

With the money from her book she was able to leave New Orleans, return to New York, find a cottage on the beach in Staten Island, and pursue the career of a serious writer. At twenty-eight, she was anxious to settle down, to test decisively her literary ability, and, for the first time, to build a home for herself. She lived in the Staten Island cottage for four years. In retrospect, one evening late in her life, when she was seventy-two, she connected her literary ambition with the sea.

I was born within sight of the Brooklyn Bridge, and I remember my mother telling us how much she enjoyed the sight of the Pacific Ocean. I also remember how much she enjoyed walking along the shore of Lake Michigan, and I can hear her now saying that she

could never live in a city where there is no water nearby. Bread and
water—what Christ knew we all need. For me water is a reminder
of Him. But I didn't have such thoughts when I was in my twenties. As I look back, I can remember how often I would seek the
water in New York City, in Chicago, in New Orleans. All the days
and months blur, but not the sight in my mind of Lake Michigan and the Atlantic Ocean and the Hudson River and the East
River and the Mississippi River and the Potomac River—the comfort of seeing water. Even when I was in Washington for a few
days, to picket and march, I wanted to see the river. No wonder
I started to write near the ocean.

These thoughts seemed to make her feel at once detached from
her past and amused by it. As I pressed her for details about that
period in her life, however, she became cranky, impatient, and returned to the image of "water" coming up yet again.

You're asking me for dates and for the names of people, and that's
not what matters. If you want to think of me in my twenties, think
of someone drifting—I won't deny it—but drifting on water.
I hadn't asked *whose* water until I was in my late twenties, not seriously; but I do recall looking at the driftwood I'd see along the
Staten Island shore and thinking of myself. Being near the ocean
gave me strength to go through the motions of living, even when
I was feeling lost and alone during difficult times.

By 1925 she was in love again, with a man who, although he was
more stable and worthy of her than her former lovers, would in his
own way cause her "difficult times." Forster, as she referred to him
in her writing and in conversations (his last name was Batterham)
was a biologist, an anarchist, and not least, an atheist. Theirs was
"a common-law marriage," she said in *The Long Loneliness*. She had
been introduced to him by his sister Lily, who was the writer Kenneth Burke's first wife. Born in North Carolina, Batterham had a

radical, agrarian sensibility: their politics were compatible. For several years they were happy together, but she then wanted a child. He was gloomy about the world's prospects and had no interest in seeing, through his own offspring, another generation struggle to make things better. When Sacco and Vanzetti were sent to the electric chair, he was devastated, went into a deep depression, and was convinced that what had happened to them was a definitive statement of how people behave toward one another. In Dorothy Day's words, admittedly spoken from a half century's distance, "The execution of those two men, who were such fighters for the poor and who were so eloquent—for Forster it was as if all the decency in the world had been killed with them."

By then, however, Forster had become a parent. Their daughter, Tamar Teresa, was born in March 1927. Before her birth they had been very much a part of New York's radical and literary world. So many of their friends now are recognized as "famous," but at the time they were, like Dorothy Day herself, struggling hard to become novelists or poets, to change the world through polemical writing or political action: Hart Crane, Allen Tate, Caroline Gordon, and of course, Malcolm Cowley, John Dos Passos, Eugene O'Neill, Mike Gold, and Kenneth Burke. All those names, and others, appear in *The Long Loneliness* A few years away from her death, Dorothy Day would look back at her words, her mention of these friendships, with unflinching self-scrutiny.

We were all friends, and we shared a lot of our hopes and our troubles with each other. When I read some of my words, though [in *The Long Loneliness*], or when the young people start asking me about those days, and all the "people" I knew, I feel uncomfortable; I feel as if I've been a terrible name-dropper. I once asked a priest to forgive me for name-dropping. He asked what I meant. I told him. He laughed, and he said it sounded to him as if I was just remembering some old friends of mine. I *was* doing that, yes; but there were other friends, and I didn't mention them. When I told the priest that, he wasn't too impressed. He said I'm a writer and I was "sharing" something with my readers. Yes, I answered, but two words just came out of me before I knew what was happening, and suddenly I heard them, to my surprise and shame: "my pride!"

Tamar Teresa was born eight months before her mother's thirtieth birthday. Dorothy Day wrote a much admired article describing the birth of her baby for *New Masses*; she was a happy as she had ever been. On the other hand, Forster was far from exultant. A thoroughly decent man, he still loved Dorothy and was not about to turn his back on their daughter. Yet he soon began to realize that it was not only parenthood to which he had to accommodate himself. First, his daughter was baptized in the Catholic church in July of 1927, when she was a few months old; then Dorothy Day became increasingly interested in that church herself. She and Forster separated for good in late December, when she asked to be baptized in the Catholic church. "I think I realized on the day I was baptized," she once said, "how long I had been waiting for that moment—all my life." In fact, she believed her life had just begun, though many of her friends thought quite the contrary.

In any case, she was going to live differently for the remaining fifty-three years of her life. She left Staten Island with her infant daughter and moved into an apartment on West Fourteenth Street "in order to be near Our Lady of Guadalupe Church." Always a reader of novels and social or political essays, she now read philosophy and theology as well. She had found a confessor, Father Zachary, and she turned to him almost daily. She was not only a Catholic, but a Catholic who wanted to learn how to live her life according to the teachings of Jesus Christ, whom the church claims as its founder. Put differently, her conversion was not nominal.

In the months and years that followed, however, Dorothy Day continued to wonder what she ought to be doing, how she ought to spend the time she had been given on this earth. She still went to the theater often and was especially taken with the performances of

Eva Le Gallienne's troupe. She kept seeing her old friends. Still the social activist, concerned about the poor, and worried about the hate in this world between races and nations, she got a job working with the Fellowship of Reconciliation. She wrote a play that elicited the interest of a number of New York directors and producers and, eventually, some Hollywood people. Though it was never produced, she was given a contract with Pathé and went to Hollywood, where she worked as a filmwriter for a while. It was not a world she could stomach, however, and she soon left for Mexico, staying with a friend in Mexico City for several months. She liked living in Mexico—the warmth, the casual but omnipresent Catholicism. But Tamar fell sick, and they hurried back to New York.

It was the time of the Great Depression, and she could not ignore what she saw around her everywhere—the widespread poverty and pain of men and women who walked the streets hoping for a job, a handout, anything. As she watched so many people endure humiliation and jeopardy, she began to wonder why the major institutions of the nation were unwilling, she believed, to respond to the need for food, shelter, and clothing. America was a rich and powerful nation, and in New York, as well as in other American cities, she had seen how much wealth was available: blocks and blocks of fancy town houses and apartment houses and stores and churches, including Catholic ones, to which came flocks of well-dressed, well-fed parishioners. She could not simply accept the disparities of "the facts of life." She read the Bible and went to church every day; she read papal encyclicals or books devoted to Catholic social teaching, and she felt that Christ's words, His example, and His admonitions had somehow been forgotten, even by priests and nuns, bishops and cardinals.

Her response was not to turn on the church, but rather to pray for it, as she prayed for her friends and for herself. Moreover, she was only too aware of her own confusions and the mistakes she had made in her personal life. She worried that her moral outrage would consume her, turning her into a bitter or smugly self-righteous person:

I remember those days, before I met Peter Maurin: I was on the brink of losing my faith, having just become a Catholic. I was very upset by what I saw—the church's apparent indifference to so much suffering. In [the early years of the Depression] people walked the streets, hundreds and hundreds of them, looking dazed and bewildered. They had no work. They had no place to go. Some groups tried to help them, but neither the state nor the church seemed as alarmed as my "radical" friends.

In *The Long Loneliness*, speaking of those friends and their activities on behalf of the poor, she made this observation: "There was Catholic membership in all these groups, of course, but no Catholic leadership. It was that very year [1929] that Pope Pius XI said sadly to Canon Cardijn, who was organizing workers in Belgium, 'The workers of the world are lost to the Church.' "

She would never forget that papal statement. It can be said that her entire life from 1932 until her death was dedicated to working against its assumptions. It was in November of 1932 that she learned of a "hunger march" to Washington, an effort to make known loudly and clearly to the nation's leaders what was happening to millions of its citizens. She had, by then, written many pieces for *Commonweal*, a liberal Catholic magazine, and she wanted very much to record what happened to the hundreds who assembled in Union Square, her old political haunt, in order to take their cause to the steps of America's Capitol Building. She was working on a second novel, one she called a social novel, a story meant to convey the everyday experiences of down-and-out, jobless people. Her trip to Washington would interrupt that writing, but she was glad for such an interruption.

While in Washington, on December 8, 1932, saddened and angered by what she saw in Union Square, on the way to Washington, and in that city—a small army of desperately impoverished and vulnerable people who were pleading for food, for a chance to work, to assert their dignity as citizens—she went to the National Shrine of the Immaculate Conception at Catholic University and prayed with all her heart and soul for a chance to "use what talents" she could find within herself for her "fellow workers, for the poor." On her return to New York City she found a man named Peter Maurin waiting for her. George M. Shuster, then *Commonweal*'s editor, had come to know Maurin, and of course had admired his contributor Dorothy Day for some time. He recognized their similarity of views and shared willingness to mix religion and politics as activists. Maurin was quick to accept Shuster's suggestion that he meet Dorothy Day, talk with her, and determine with her what might be done on behalf of the poor.

For days that became weeks and then months, the two of them talked, trying to figure out what each might do to change the dismal contemporary American scene for the better. Gradually Dorothy got to know Peter, learning enough about him to realize what an extraordinary person he was and how congenially he and she were able to work together.

On many occasions Dorothy made it quite clear that for her Peter's "spirit and ideas" were utterly essential to the rest of her life. She was inspired by his struggle to make the principles of Jesus incarnate in the kind of life he lived, to rescue them from those who had turned Him into an icon of Sunday convenience. The Catholic Worker Movement became their shared initiative.

The newspaper came first, of course: they were both writers. On May Day 1933 the two of them had 2,500 copies of *The Catholic Worker* available for distribution. They had not opened an office, hired a staff, secured mailing lists, or planned elaborate promotion. They had raised $57 from two priests and a nun and from their own almost empty pockets, and with the help of a printer had put out what Dorothy Day would later describe as a "small eight-page sheet the size of *The Nation*." Then came the attempt to attract readers, by a long march from the Lower East Side to Union Square, where they joined the political crowds assembled there and peddled their paper, no doubt to the surprise of many onlookers, for whom the juxtaposition of "Catholic" and "worker" seemed anomalous.

In a way, as Dorothy Day herself once put it, "the rest was history." She was not being grandiose, as she made clear by her immediate qualifications. "I mean by 'history' the history of all of us who have been part of the Catholic Worker family. That's what happened, that's what we became, a family spread across all the cities and states of this country." Within a few years, *The Catholic Worker* had a circulation of over a hundred and fifty thousand, with many more readers than that figure suggests, because it has always been a paper that is handed from person to person. It is a monthly which, to this day, sells for "a penny a copy."

Yet Dorothy Day and Peter Maurin were not content simply to write about what they believed the Catholic church has to offer the ordinary worker, to publish their moral and political philosophy. They both believed in the importance of "works." Together they founded the hospitality houses that became part of the American social scene for men and women who had no other place to go, nothing to eat, and were at the mercy of whatever secular or religious charity happened to be available. Peter Maurin envisioned a twentieth-century version of the ancient notion of a hospice, a place where "works of mercy" were offered and acknowledged in a person-to-person fashion, as opposed to the faceless, bureaucratic procedures of the welfare state. He shared that vision with Dorothy Day. Together they started to make that vision real, by renting a store, an apartment, buying bread and butter, making coffee, preparing soup, serving food to the homeless, finding clothes for them, offering them, when possible, a place to sleep, and very important, sitting with them, trying to converse, hoping in some way to offer them friendship and affection. Other people joined to help, and in time there would be over thirty "houses of hospitality" across the nation. Over the years more have started, folded, and sometimes got going again.

The Catholic Worker has dwelt often on the moral as well as political significance of agriculture. Beyond its obvious purpose of growing food, it is also an antidote to the alienation caused by industrialism, which separates us from the bare bones of life and makes us spend entire lives in offices or on assembly lines. Farms were built up by the men and women and children who became part of the Catholic Worker family in New England and New York State, in Appalachia, in the Midwest, and on the Pacific Coast. In all those places knots of kindred souls became centers of action. Newspapers appeared in Chicago, Buffalo, St. Louis, Seattle, Houston, Los Angeles, and as far away as England and Australia. There was no party line, no set of rules or positions handed down to the various hospitality houses or farms or newspapers. Thousands of men and women the world over responded in various ways to the example and determination of two Catholic laypersons, Dorothy Day and Peter Maurin.

From May Day 1933 until November 29, 1980, when she died, Dorothy Day lived without interruption as a Catholic Worker. She edited the paper of that name, she lived in the hospitality houses of that name, and she traveled by bus across the United States, teaching and speaking, helping to cook, and sitting with people the rest of us call bums or homeless or drunks. She also kept saying her prayers, going through devotional rhythms, reading and rereading the books she loved, and writing her *Catholic Worker* column, "On Pilgrimage." Tamar grew up at her side, then left, married, and made her mother a grandmother numerous times.

During those years Dorothy Day took on many a controversy. She stood up to Franco when he started the Spanish Civil War, thereby losing lots of Catholic readers who saw Franco as a godsend who was leading a Catholic charge against the atheists, the Communists who had taken over Spain. She argued the case for pacifism during the Second World War, a lonely stance, indeed, and one that many of her closest friends, her most enthusiastic coworkers adamantly rejected. After the war, she continued her work among the poor and on behalf of those whom we now call minorities. (One of the first efforts she and Peter Maurin made was in Harlem, at the very start of their work together.) I well remember her, during the 1960s, riding buses in the South, involving herself in the civil rights struggle, and showing up on the West Coast alongside Cesar Chavez. By then she was a veteran of marches and demonstrations and picket lines and jails, someone who had learned to live simply, travel lightly. Wherever she was, she found time every day for prayer, for reading the Bible, for attending Mass, taking Communion, and saying confession.

The last time I saw her, not long before her death, I had taken a group of my students to the Catholic Worker office, to St. Joseph's House, and to Maryhouse, where she lived. She was frail, but she stood straight and was as gracious as she had been years earlier, when she had the strength to serve personally the hundreds of homeless people who came daily to the Catholic Worker kitchen for soup and coffee and bread. We shared a few memories, and I asked her what she was reading and whether she was doing any writing. She was reading, yet again, her beloved Tolstoy—"The Death of Ivan Ilyich"—and Dickens—*Little Dorrit*. Her eyes were full of life, no matter the diminished capacity of her lungs, the compromised exertions of her heart muscles. "It will soon be over," she told me, then added,

I try to think back; I try to remember this life that the Lord gave me; the other day I wrote down the words "a life remembered," and I was going to try to make a summary for myself, write what mattered most—but I couldn't do it. I just sat there and thought of our Lord, and His visit to us all those centuries ago, and I said to myself that my great luck was to have had Him on my mind for so long in my life!

I heard the catch in her voice as she spoke, and soon her eyes were a little moist, but she quickly started talking of her great love for Tolstoy, as if, thereby, she had changed the subject.

II.

Lives That Say, Sing, and Show

James Agee

I n his senior year at Harvard, James Agee and some of his *Advocate* friends did a brilliant parody of *Time*, then only a few years old. One of Agee's best friends, Dwight Macdonald, was working on another Luce magazine, *Fortune*. Agee did not exactly have the best prospects at graduation in 1932, with the Depression in full sway. The *Time* parody probably helped Macdonald get him a job at *Fortune*, thereby launching a journalistic career of almost two decades. In 1933 Agee was a New Yorker—in the borough of Manhattan, that is. He worked in a new skyscraper, the Chrysler Building, on the fifty-second floor. His habits as a *Fortune* essayist have become a part of the awesome reputation that clings to him still, more than a half-century after his death. Agee and his Beethoven symphonies blasting away through the night, with the lighted streets of the world's greatest city far below. Agee and coffee, Agee and booze, Agee and the typewriter, Agee and cigarettes, and most important, Agee and deadlines—which seemed with him to take on a literal meaning. He drove himself ruthlessly and experienced terrible spells of apprehension and despair as he contested time and his superiors, not to mention his own exacting conscience, in a (usually) desperate effort to turn in finished copy before it was too late.

But for all the drama, if not histrionics, the articles by and large got done; invariably they were brilliantly constructed, witty, informative, entertaining. Here was a poet harnessed to the things of this commercial world and somehow able to sing well indeed for his supper. He wrote of rugs and roads and railroads. He wrote of flowers and towns and quinine cartels and commodities speculators. He was able to mobilize within himself the dispassionate curiosity of the reporter, and when linked to the storyteller's eye for detail the result was superb journalistic narrative. Just below the surface, though, was a strong moral sensibility, held in check by the constraints of the Luce empire, but never banished outright—even when the subject was as innocuous as strawberries: "In England, behind walls of a respectable age, strawberries are still served at Solemn High Tea. In England this June the school tuckshop will be clamorous with hard-hatted little Harrovians absorbing 'dringers,' a somewhat lily-gilding mixture of fresh strawberries and strawberry ice cream."

This and more was served to us in an English course I took at college, when Agee was a name I was yet to know. We were told, as Agee may have told himself, that any crop, fruit or vegetable or cereal or so-called raw material, can open up whatever doors the writer wishes. Strawberries took Agee to the privileged realms of England's so-called public schools—an indirect reminder to *Fortune's* wealthy that while millions could take no meal, however meager, for granted, a small group of kids, not especially prone to modesty or self-criticism, were making an innocent strawberry an object of scandal. Soon, in 1936, there would be cotton, the staple crop of the American South's sharecropper and tenant farm agriculture. It was this assignment that took Agee to Alabama, and the result would be a long, memorable personal and moral struggle, as well as a book, *Let Us Now Praise Famous Men*, which is Agee's single most significant piece of writing—the only book of his, arguably, that will continue to be connected with those banal adjectives *great* and *classic* over the generations.

Agee went to Alabama to a small farming community between Montgomery and Birmingham during the summer of 1936, an election year. The Depression was becoming a way of life. Strong federal efforts by the Roosevelt administration softened considerably many of the edges of extreme poverty and unemployment, but the country's economic system, everyone agreed, was still quite sick. Few were harder off than the South's farmers, black and white. At the time *Fortune* was not about to do an article on the region's rural black people. For that matter, Agee and Evans were not sent down to do a searching documentary even of the wretched circumstances bedeviling white yeomen in rural Alabama, among other parts of Dixie. Cotton was king, still, and an economic analysis of that particular royal condition, colorfully written, was what Agee's bosses had in mind.

For him, however, this was an opportunity of the greatest import: a way of drawing upon interests he came by as a Southern boy; a way, too, of exploring not only an economic problem but the moral aspects of a nation's life; a way of escaping Manhattan's cosmopolitan culture to pursue that elusive honesty, purity, and integrity so many of us keep looking for, around corner after corner of our lives. And he was to work with Walker Evans, a friend of similarly conflicted temperament: anxious to pursue Art, willing to break rules to do so, stubbornly independent, of broad sensibility, and not beyond the inclination to call upon bourbon as a dear, helpful friend.

They stayed in Alabama over a month, July and into August. They lived with three families and tried to understand, deeply and respectfully, their everyday existence. They failed in their assigned mission; *Fortune* would never show its readers, through Agee's words and Evans's photographs, the human aspect, so to speak, of cotton production. The photographs that appear in *Let Us Now Praise Famous Men* are not really meant to be a part of work done at the behest of the Farm Security Administration, which employed Evans during the 1930s. Evans's pictures show not only terribly hurt, perplexed, and vulnerable people but scenes, interior and exterior, worthy of an artist's careful and controlled recognition. For Evans, an old pair of country shoes, a chair and broom, or a linoleum-covered kitchen table were opportunities not for the muckraking or polemical mind but for the unashamedly observing eye of a particular kind of artist.

Evans and Agee in the South were two well-bred and well-educated young men, each in search of a career in one of the arts. There was not much time for them to figure out in detail, never mind argumentatively, what their ultimate purposes were. They were guests. They were obliged to follow the rhythms of others— extremely harassed people, living under a hot sun, moneyless, and with no great expectation of doing very well in the world.

Agee was as hungry in his own way, as confused and uncertain and apprehensive, as his hosts. They were up at dawn and ready for bed shortly after sundown, tired from hard, demanding agricultural labor. He was up with them, trying to learn the details of their days and their ways—but driven, one realizes, by a strong conscience determined this time to have its say and then some. The seething, anarchic rebelliousness that had hitherto (at Exeter and Harvard and in Manhattan) taken an erratic course—now apparent in sarcasm or satire or parody, now buried under layers of religious sentiment or literary analysis—began at last to emerge as a full-fledged moral force. It was as if Agee heard a voice within saying something like this, loud and clear: here you are, close to the proud and hurt Appalachian people of your childhood, close to the people your Lord Jesus Christ kept mentioning, kept keeping near at hand, kept attempting to heal and feed and comfort; so you had best take exceeding care, you who are good with words, you who have been quick to turn on others, the hypocrites and pretenders and sycophants, the self-absorbed tastemakers of a world very far, socially and culturally, from north-central Alabama.

Under such personal circumstances, it is small wonder that an apparently routine *Fortune* assignment turned out to be the most challenging and frustrating task Agee would ever have to confront. When he got back he went with his second wife, Alma, to a small town in New Jersey, where he took on, it seemed, not only Alabama's injustices but the whole world's. And his efforts to describe what he saw were similarly monumental—as if the college student who admired James Joyce hoped to make out of a Southern scene what Joyce had made of Dublin. Nor was this effort one Agee would ever feel satisfied with. It is safe to say that he ultimately surrendered and reluctantly allowed a portion of his labored, intense, tormented prose to emerge as the book we know as *Let Us Now Praise Famous Men*. Even to call it that, a book, is to tread on the writer's infinitely (it seems) sensitive toes: "This is a *book* only by necessity," he insisted. More seriously, "it is an effort in human actuality, in which the reader is no less centrally involved than the authors and those of whom they tell."

Agee was himself a great performer—a mimic, a scold, a man capable of large, defiant, and self-wounding gestures. He had the dramatist's interest in the great audience of others, and he wanted from them a kind of engagement worthy of his own high theatricality. *Let Us Now Praise Famous Men* can in fact be regarded as a moral drama, a long prose poem structured as a dramatic presentation. We begin with "persons and places," a dramatis personae of sorts. There are "verses," a "preamble," a quotation from *King Lear*, a section called "Intermission: Conversation in the Lobby," and a section described as "Inductions." The author wants to tell us about essentials, things like money and shelter and clothing and education and work, but he is constantly searching for ways to turn such topics into an edifying spectacle, with protagonists, confrontations, rising action, and a compelling denouement or two. Agee's chief enemy was that of every ambitious moral writer—the potential boredom of the proudly well-intentioned reader, for whom *Let Us Now Praise Famous Men* would provide merely a vivid account of a problem, namely, 1930s Southern tenantry.

He had plenty of doubt and sarcasm to hand out, and one gets the impression that no political party, no idea become a "movement" would achieve immunity from the skeptical part of his mind. The danger, needless to say, is captiousness—a chronic insistence,

all-or-none fashion, that various political leaders or social move-
ments, or writers for that matter, either pass full muster or submit
to withering, continual criticism. At times, Agee falls victim to his
own scruples—turning ironic bitterness or snide contempt or outright scorn on a wide spectrum of individuals: on Franklin D. Roosevelt and his New Deal for instance, on the teachers of the rural
South, black and white alike, on New York intellectuals, even on the
reader. The *reader*, a catchall designation if ever there was one, gets
swiped at by, of all people, a writer who worries about "the average
reader's tendency to label." But Agee was nothing if not self-critical.
He knew the reader and labeler in himself, working in conjunction
with the reactively humble writer, still unable to overcome pride, the
sin of sins.

Such self-criticism is scarcely a guarantee of absolution. Mea
culpa can be a sly form of arrogance or a canny means of curry-
ing favor, enlisting the reader's sympathy on behalf of an earnestly
disarming breast-beater who turns out to be, in the clutch, quite
capable of a cleverly effective self-defense.

I have used this book of his in my courses, and I have heard the
confusion expressed vigorously: sincere annoyance, plaintive cries
for interpretive assistance, angry shrugs, or straightforward contempt. Nor is the teacher always grateful for the student who becomes ecstatic about Agee's writing and its various postures. While
his writing has a kind of transcendence, a great, dramatic, daring
lift upward—away from all the petty, self-serving, uncritical ones
who live on campuses or in various commercial offices—and while
he can disarm one utterly with the sweetness of his talk and his compelling evocation of a complex kind of compassion, he is at the same
time a very angry writer who wants an engagement with the rest of
us, a joint willingness to say no, to say wait, to say stop, to say, even,
enough!

His inconsistencies, near to contradictions, are worthy of the
novelist, resulting in marvelous descriptions of people, places, and
events. His lyrical gifts show themselves over and over again in

touching, even stunning, moments in which the ordinary (earth, flowers, furniture, buildings) is rendered miraculous. "Behind the house," we are told, "the dirt is blond and bare, except a little fledging of grass-leaves at the roots of structures, and walked-out rags of grass thickening along the sides."

On the other hand, Agee has by no means contented himself with close, pastoral cataloguing or even with good storytelling, as when he turns a sleepless night into the hellish experience it was, with a hot, sweaty, city-spoiled visitor struggling desperately to deal with bugs and ticks and flies and mosquitoes. We get to know some Alabama people of the 1930s "right well," as they might have put it. But there are other more confounded pages, like a section titled "Education," in which the author is a social critic with, literally, a vengeance. His anger is boundless in that chapter, and it spills from Alabama to just about everywhere. And shaking his fists hard and often, he naturally risks losing his grip on logic. Agee tells us at one point, for instance, that " 'Education' as it stands is tied in with every bondage" he can think of; he goes on to say that it "is the chief cause of these bondages." Mere rhetoric one suspects, or a bloated version of what education is, and does, and is able to do. Agee himself claimed to have learned rather a lot at St. Andrews, at Exeter, and at Harvard, from teachers whom he mentions with considerable thankfulness and praise in *Permit Me Voyage*. He came to Alabama a thoroughly educated young man, no matter the flaws in the schools he attended. The families he visited in the South didn't quite need the kind of burden he places on them of being virtuous innocents, who ought to be protected from the corruptions of something called "Education." Nor need their human dignity be used as a foil by one of a relative handful lucky enough during the Depression to be able to obtain an Exeter and Harvard education.

Agee loved the people he met. He also felt, and acknowledged feeling, terribly guilty while with them; he was, after all, the lucky, privileged outsider, soon enough back in Manhattan, playing Beethoven's Ninth Symphony in a room with a majestic view of, well, New York City's ghettos, as a matter of fact, among other neighborhoods. He wanted to hold up his new (temporary) friends as honorable and decent people. But he was with them rather briefly, and there must have been an element of restraint on all sides, as hosts and guests fumbled toward some reasonable trust. Still, one doubts Agee saw and heard all there was to see and hear—and he knew, of course, that such was the case. In a year, in two years, there still might have been secrets not discovered, though as a rule the more time people spend together, the better they get to know one another. The point is that Agee spent much less time than he knew would be reasonably adequate—and that fact only added to self-recrimination already bordering on self-flagellation.

Going through *Let Us Now Praise Famous Men*, one begins to notice, not surprisingly, that such responses and conclusions lead the writer to the edge of despair, if not to its very center. Agee's sort of mission is bound to push the mind hard. If we are, that is, to follow the advice of Shakespeare or of those nineteenth-century political revolutionaries who wanted to overthrow various despots (leaving aside what history would give us as the consequence), then we had best be prepared to deal with the moral anger that goes along with such moral analysis, namely, the kind meant to prompt social change. And anger craves objects.

Agee is continually self-lacerating, but he rouses himself at critical times to a fierce, sometimes surprising assault on a wide range of others. In the section "Money," he begins with a remark of Franklin Delano Roosevelt's during one of his campaigns: "You are farmers; I am a farmer myself." We are then yanked down to Alabama, to learn about the finances of some impossibly poor farmers, with whom the squire of New York State's Hyde Park, overlooking the Hudson River, has declared his occupational solidarity. The effect, of course, is achieved: devastating irony. The reader is brought up short, confronted through the disarming use of a quotation with all sorts of uncomfortable facts and thoughts, not least the glibness of liberal rhetoric viewed from a certain vantage point. What is one to say? Did not Roosevelt try hard, extremely hard, all during the 1930s, and against great opposition, to alleviate the distress of America's poor farm people? If the mental and moral life of tenant farmers is worth painstaking consideration, as in *Let Us Now Praise Famous Men*, are we to dismiss the political struggle of the 1930s waged by Franklin Delano Roosevelt, among others, and all because of a cleverly placed quotation taken out of the context of a given speech, never mind a campaign? What can be said in defense of what seems like a blatantly cheap shot?

Agee would, no doubt, laugh if not sneer at such a series of questions. He was a writer responding to a given set of circumstances and making all sorts of connections so as to agitate other minds to thought, even as his own had been awakened and moved to cry, sing, perform. If while he contemplated rural Alabama, a line or two spoken by an American president in the 1930s struck Agee's fancy, then so be it. His job, as a poet, novelist, and literary essayist, was not detailed political analysis (either with respect to farm labor or reformist national politics), nor for that matter psychiatric analysis; it was not even cool, documentary exposition or logical argument.

Not that Agee didn't come up with his own rather vigorous apology of sorts for an occasional misstep:

> I am not at all trying to lay out a thesis, far less to substantiate or solve. I do not consider myself qualified. I know only that murder is being done, against nearly every individual on the planet, and that there are dimensions and correlations of cure which not only are not being used but appear to be scarcely considered or suspected. I know there is cure, even now available, if only it were available, in science and in the fear and joy of God. This is only a brief personal statement of these convictions: and my self-disgust is less in my ignorance, and far less in my "failure" to "defend" or "support" the statement, than in my inability to state it even so far as I see it, and in my inability to blow out the brains with it of you who take what it is talking of lightly, or not seriously enough.

He is writing, then, in a nonacademic tradition, even an anti-academic one. He does not advertise himself as a field-worker, and certainly not as a social scientist. Nor is he a journalist reporting in the factual or muckraking traditions—or, at least, not *only* such a writer. There are, definitely, reportorial aspects to the book. But this is the book, mainly, of an unashamed moralist, who happens also to be a man often marvelously exact and discerning in his use of words. It is the book, too, of a mind reared in twentieth-century techno-logical hope, edged by a lingering Christian vision, not at all trium-phant yet not acknowledged with mere lip service either. There are, once again, the strenuous assaults on the author's own worth, a bit startling, given his membership in an intelligentsia more apt to turn its criticism on others or to define the tendency to self-criticism as evidence of psychological illness.

As for his regret that he hasn't quite been able to "blow out the brains" of various readers with the truculent assertions he has worked into a deliberately discordant and unwieldy book, it would be unwise to ignore the remark as a foolish and regrettable instance of hyper-bole. Agee's rebellion, Walker Evans insisted from the retrospective vantage point of 1960, was "unquenchable, self-damaging, deeply principled, infinitely costly, and ultimately priceless." The princi-pled voice of Agee's was not easily shed; it sets the tone for a lot of his writing, and the rebellion Evans mentions was part of a particular religious tradition. The Judeo-Christian principles, after all, which prompted such dedicated rage in Agee were stated first by an angry Jeremiah, an angry Isaiah, and in the New Testament by a Jesus suddenly not meek and accepting but full of scorn and disgust as he confronts the arid pietism of the Temple.

When Agee talks of "murder," he is once again flirting with hy-perbole, or so we might think, and when he says that this murder is being committed "against nearly every individual on the planet," we may well want to know precisely what he means. Who is doing the killing, and with what in mind? And when we are told that a *cure* is available but is not being "considered or suspected," we have reached a logical impasse.

What does the author want—empathy, sympathy, understanding shouted from all available rooftops? A stint of time in Alabama in an effort to help others with their various problems? How long a spell, as a matter of fact, since Agee himself was gone in August of 1936, having arrived in July? And doing what: teaching in schools the author condemns so bitterly, helping in the fields when no help is really required? Cash: is that the answer, a philanthropic inundation? The people Agee knew might have generously responded to that last question, with undisguised, unmodified enthusiasm. But one wonders what pitch of skeptical scorn might then have been forthcoming from a writer so contemptuous of the material side of American capitalism, even while he lived off it as a writer and before that as a student at a wealthy school and an even wealthier college.

The question persists, therefore: what kind of seriousness did the author have in mind for us, if he is not to shoot us through the head? I fear there is no clear answer to this question. There remains, inevitably, the reader's sense that he or she is being hit hard with rhetoric and that maybe the best thing to do is proceed, turn the page, and hope for some further acquaintance with Alabama's people or even for a few more jabs at the reader's assumed complacency.

Or is this to be unnecessarily or gratuitously tough, crabbed, and mean-spirited about the book? Maybe so. I have tried to read a paragraph of Agee's fairly closely, assuming that someone who spent three or four years working on the writing, each sentence a struggle, we are told, ought to be attended to rather faithfully; but I have done so without the blanket approval of a fellow traveler, to use that expression in a more literal rather than symbolic or idiomatic sense, since I have talked, as Agee did, with families and worked with them for a number of years in the rural South, Alabama included. Nor have I been consistent over the years in my own sentiments about Agee's book. There was a time when it was scripture to me, every word and idea a heavenly gift.

Let Us Now Praise Famous Men was reissued in 1960, a generation's time after its first publication in 1941, at which point it received a decidedly mixed critical response and a singularly poor one with respect to buyers. In 1941, the Great Depression was finally receding; the prospect of America's involvement in a second World War was accomplishing what no federal recovery program had been able to do. By 1960, however, an altogether different climate of opinion was fast developing. A war had been fought and won; a cold war had begun. America, or at least a segment of it, was prospering. But by the late 1950s there were, as they say, a few problems; one of them turned out to be an entire region of the country—the South. With its racial conflict, with its severe, unremitting rural poverty, the South had scarcely been affected by the social and economic improvements many other Americans had come to take for granted. In 1954, the Supreme Court sent a strong signal to the South; in 1956, an extremely reluctant President Eisenhower had to send federal troops there; by 1957, Rosa Parks had taken her stand in Montgomery, Alabama, saying *enough*! to segregationist laws that told the people of that state and its neighbors where to sit, stand, eat, and learn. A hitherto unknown minister, Dr. Martin Luther King, Jr., leader of a Montgomery, Alabama, Baptist Church, was quickly at Rosa Park's side and would soon become an important national leader. The election of 1960 gave us the youngest president in American history, ready and willing to bring new energy to political life—though possibly no more prepared than most other Americans to deal with the sudden tide of social change that was given dramatic impetus in early February of 1960 when four black students asked to be served at the food counter of a Woolworth store in Greensboro, North Carolina. It was therefore an especially opportune time for Houghton Mifflin to give the public, a whole new generation of Americans, a chance to meet James Agee and Walker

Evans and the fellow citizens the two of them had met a quarter of a century earlier.

I remember not only buying *Let Us Now Praise Famous Men* at that time but seeing many others do so. I remember finding copies of the book, in hardcover no less, all over the South. And I especially remember copies of the book in Freedom Houses, as we called them in the summer of 1964, during the Mississippi Summer Project, an effort by young Americans of both races to bring voter registration to the steadfastly segregationist Delta. In Canton, Mississippi; in Greenwood, Mississippi; in Yazoo City, Mississippi; on a table, on the floor, on a bed, on a chair; read by white, well-to-do students from Ivy League colleges but read as well by black students from the North and from the South it was a bible of sorts, at least for a while, a sign, a symbol, a reminder, an eloquent testimony that others had cared, had gone forth to look and hear, and had come back to stand up and address their friends and neighbors and those beyond personal knowing.

I often wondered why some of the blacks I knew in SNCC (the Student Nonviolent Coordinating Committee, a major organization involved in the Civil Rights struggle of the early 1960s) had such favorable words for Agee's books, along with strong reservations, which grew stronger as those same blacks withdrew increasingly from a cooperative effort with whites into the insistent position of "black power." Here, for example, is a black youth from Tuscaloosa (not all that far from the Alabama territory Agee stalked) reflecting on "*the* book," as he kept calling it:

To me, the proof of the truth in Agee's writing is that he makes mistakes, big ones. I mean, for a black, the big moment is in that small section called "Near a Church," where he's with his buddy Walker Evans, I believe, and they're getting the camera set up, and they see a Negro couple, and I guess Evans wants to photograph them, but whatever the couple has on their minds, Agee is walking behind them, and he disturbs them. They hear him and look, and he gets closer, and they freeze, they just freeze: who is this white guy, and what in hell is he going to do to us? Pretty fast, Agee sees the whole lousy situation: the young Negro couple, scared to death, and he wanting to be nice and friendly, but knowing there was no way, no way, not even for him, big and easy with words, to dissolve the crazy, terrible stuff that was going on between them and him and his buddy. The two young Negroes stare at him. They just stare. I guess he stared back. Talk about fear!

Agee's own description of the scene goes like this: "They just kept looking at me. There was no more for them to say than for me. The least I could have done was to throw myself flat on my face and embrace and kiss their feet. That impulse took hold of me so powerfully, from my whole body, not by thought, that I caught myself from doing it exactly and as scarcely as you snatch yourself from jumping from a sheer height. . . ." He knew he would, indeed, be thought loony, or a sinister confidence man, up to some mischief. Blacks, back then, had to put up with all sorts of white craziness in terror-struck or bitter or mocking silence. But what are we to make of the somewhat overwrought impulse of self-abasement that drives Agee so close to its active expression? Is he, with a good storyteller's narrative impulse, exaggerating for dramatic purposes? Is he pushing us, morally and psychologically both, and educating us as well—here is what goes on down South, and here is how we ought to feel? Might he be dismissed as the archetypal bleeding-heart liberal? Why did he bother that couple, who only wanted their privacy? *That* question might, of course, be applied to the entire expedition, a kind of raid on the vulnerability of the poor white folk interviewed and photographed and portrayed as down-and-out objects of pity for countless others rich enough to buy books.

Agee's book *Let Us Now Praise Famous Men* is a great one precisely because it prompts such moral and social questions about the responsibilities of the various observers, investigators, and writers who make their way into this or that community in hopes of discovering something, doing documentary work, finding material for an article, story, or book. How much can one get to know about people in a few days, a week or two, or a month, as a "guest" of theirs, a visitor with a deadline in mind? What matters are *not* discussed, even looked into, by those of us who do fieldwork, learning as we go from home to home certain limits of conversation? How ought one to behave in that field, with what degree of tact, reticence, and respect for the privacy of others? Is it exploitive to enter a neighborhood, learn certain facts, get a sense of certain attitudes, and then make a living by writing about it? Ought the writer then, at the very least, offer to split financial payment for an article or book with the people who have, after all, given their time and energy and been one's patient teachers? Or if they are not to be reimbursed personally, should something be given to a cause or organization that works with and is of help to their particular neighborhood, town, or region?

On the other hand, isn't it possible to wonder at all this fuss, this self-accusation, these declarations of personal confusion if not outright wrongdoing? James Agee was an intelligent, careful, considerate writer. He went south at the behest of an important national magazine in hopes of doing a good reporter's job and, presumably, of reaching and significantly touching a host of readers. It is hard to imagine him being rude or crude in any way; it is hard to imagine any harm he did as a visitor. Why then his nearly hysterical self-recriminations? And are the people Agee visited well served by the various literary, philosophical, and political asides—which, it can be argued, turn the situation of particular families into an occasion for James Agee's various ruminations, reflections, and diatribes?

Agee worries about *himself* a lot; he regrets the terrible discrepancies between his kind of life and the lives of others. But what were his *hosts'* worries, not to mention their wishes? Maybe one or two of them might have said something like this: look, mister Jim, take it easy and stop working yourself up into such a lather. We're not having an easy time of it, no question we're not. But we're not wringing our hands and crying and feeling sorry for ourselves, and we don't need anyone else crying for us. Sure, we'd like a better deal. Some of the things that upset you don't happen to upset us. We just want to do a little better as farmers, get better prices. We don't want you going around saying that we're sorry ones, that we're the sorriest people ever, and all we deserve is everyone's tears. We're working hard, and we'll keep working hard, and we're proud of that, not sitting around feeling glum, waiting for someone to pat us on the back and tell us they really do sympathize, you know!

I have to mention still another matter. Agee does make relatively brief but pointed mention of segregationist sentiment among some people he met in the course of his travels through Alabama, but he doesn't spell out what, if anything, his hosts had to think and say about black people. We learn a lot about what *he* feels, and after a while begin to wonder at his reticence about such an obviously significant subject—the black people, their proper situation—much discussed in the South during its long history by white people of all classes. One wonders whether Agee couldn't bear to hear, or having heard, to relay to others some of the racial attitudes of the people he got to know. Is it an outrageous generalization to assume, back in 1936, a substantial amount of racial prejudice among just about all of Alabama's white tenant farmers, not to mention its lawyers and doctors and college professors, and wouldn't the same go for plenty of the people of Illinois and New York and Massachusetts?

I remember in the march from Selma to Montgomery during the early 1960s that many ordinary white tenant farmers came and stood, and alas, had their say. I worked in three mostly rural counties of Alabama during that decade and have elsewhere (in *Migrants, Sharecroppers, Mountaineers*, which is Volume Three of *Children of Crisis*) tried to describe some of the fears and hatreds any number of men, women, and children were quite willing and indeed determined to express. When I first read *Let Us Now Praise Famous Men* in college during the early 1950s, I never stopped to ask myself about the question of race or how it had or hadn't been handled by the author. When I read the book again in the early 1960s, I couldn't stop noticing what seemed to be the disproportionate assumptions of guilt and innocence. Agee as the one who ought to feel shame, if not guilt, and the New York (or Harvard) intellectuals whose limitations were plentiful enough: here were the terrible crooks and frauds and bigots who run things in the South or the North—the schools and colleges and public institutions. And then, in sharp contrast, the hurt families Agee and Evans met, and the young black couple they met, and the badly exploited blacks they did not meet but do mention—all of these people seemingly without blemish, or relatively so. I suppose there is a degree of idealization in all of us when we leave home to see the world in the hope of rendering it justice in words. So that if we readers wonder how silly, self-important, and egotistical some of Agee's intellectual colleagues are made to appear, perhaps we ought to remember how wonderfully gentle and kind (is the word forgiving?) Agee is toward others less like himself in certain respects. He forgives some to the point where there is little forgiveness left for others.

My questions and criticism show the great strength of Agee's literary-journalistic writing, with its mixture of accurate, suggestive description, compassionate portraiture, skeptical cultural observation, and pungent social analysis, all rendered in a prose distinguished, when compared to that of other writers of documentary nonfiction, by a caring, lyrical intensity. If there is any writing of Agee's that places him, tells us what he believes deep down, it is to be found in this paragraph:

All that each person is, and experiences, and shall never experience, in body and in mind, all these things are differing expressions of himself and of one root, and are identical: and not one of these things nor one of these persons is ever quite to be duplicated, nor replaced, nor has it ever quite had precedent: but each is a new and incommunicably tender life, wounded in every breath, and almost as hardly killed as easily wounded: sustaining, for a while, without defense, the enormous assaults of the universe.

Those "assaults" did not spare his personal life. His first marriage, to Olivia Saunders, was followed in 1939 by a second one, to Alma Mailman, that did not last long. Their son, Joel, is now a writer in his own right. A third marriage, to Mia Fritsch, began in 1946 and would, in the less than ten years left to Agee, result in two daughters and one son. He had a rough time in the late 1930s while writing *Let Us Now Praise Famous Men*. Besides being constantly short of cash, he wasn't at all sure how to cope with the families he'd met or with himself, the one who saw and heard, who came and left, who writes and is read. The book was written in Frenchtown, New Jersey, and was originally called *Three Tenant Farmers*. The decision, with respect to the title, to use words from the Apocrypha—Ecclesiasticus, chapter 44—was an extremely significant one. The reader is told right from the start to contend with a moral narrative, with a literary sensibility intent on an ironic rather than a predominantly sociological angle of vision. And not surprisingly, the author's critical response to his own book is severely moral, if not moralistic.

Year after year, as I use Agee's writing in my courses and read student papers about him, I ask myself, as do they, why we bother with him and what he means to us, who are alive more than a generation after his untimely death. In my lectures I try to stress his singular gifts as a writer of English, a voice of brave and candid dissatisfaction with the way things are—the inhumanity, the injustice, the meanness and callousness, the smugness and arrogance. He was a giant of a man, with a wide-ranging, restless, hungry mind that crossed all sorts of boundaries, borders, and established limits; he was a teacher, who through poems and stories and essays made people morally uncomfortable, morally alert, more morally searching. He was not least a pilgrim. A student once sent me a note after the course was over. Only twenty, dying of leukemia, he went to lectures, read books, and wrote papers, feeling it his duty, his responsibility, as the particular person he was, to "keep going as before." In his note he had this to say about James Agee:

I expect to die in a few months. I'll be less than half as old as he was when he died. I've been reading everything of his I can get my hands on. I feel that he's the one who has the most to say to me, before I die. The reason is this: he seemed to have lived each day as if it was a gift, and as if it was his last, and he wrote that way. He makes me feel that there's reason to be proud that I'm a human being, that I can sit and read James Agee and understand what he wrote and respond to his language and his ideas. A lot of the time, after I read the newspapers or the weekly newsmagazines, or watch the news on television, I'm ashamed to be a human being, because of all the terrible things we do to one another. We make animals seem so civilized!

But with Agee, your faith is restored. He was such a good person; and he was such a wonderful writer. I'm sure he had his faults, like the rest of us. But he gets through to you. He reaches your heart, and he reaches your mind. A lot of people reach your heart, and a lot of intellectuals reach your mind, but to do both, to make you feel and make you think—and even to make you try to be a better person, that's a lot! To me, Agee is someone who knew what it meant to live in this crazy century. He only lived 45 years, but he saw it all, the wars, the nuclear madness, the depression, Hitler and Stalin. Even so, he kept his sense of humor, and he wrote those beautiful books. They tell you about yourself, because they tell you what a human being is, whether a child or a teenager, whether a poor person or a guy who tries to understand poor people, those way below him on the social ladder, and with no money at all.

There was more, including a self-deprecatory apologia worthy of Agee himself. I have kept that letter tucked in a copy of *Let Us Now Praise Famous Men*—a decent, thoughtful, dying youth's homage

to a writer with a keen and abiding sense of how fragile and tenta-
tive things are and, for that reason, how precious is this existence
allowed us. James Agee was a promising poet who never became
more than that. He was shrewd and knowing, a marvelously poi-
gnant storyteller who never became the self-assured narrator of
fiction he might have been. He never got enough beyond himself
and his given world, never attained the distance of a great novelist. He was a sharp, powerful critic of books and films, though he
never lived to become a more substantial analyst of them. He was an
utterly unique and brilliant social observer; his effort to do justice
to the Alabama world of 1936 stands apart from the entire field of
documentary writing as an example that makes the rest of us pause
with extreme modesty. He was a movie scriptwriter just beginning,
though already the enormous talent and great good humor and
magical dramatic sense were more than apparent. He was, not least,
a letter writer not only to Father Flye but to other quite remarkable
people, like Dwight Macdonald and Robert Fitzgerald—someone
who could combine friendship with continuing, contained, highly
intelligent discourse, though a less harassed, more relaxedly meditative correspondence might have been possible in a life longer than
Agee's was to be. And finally, he was a person thoroughly, completely, in every sense sui generis. Those like myself, who never
knew him, bow in respect, wince a bit with sadness, and admit quietly and regretfully the inevitable twinge of envy.

So if we mourn his premature death, we have to declare our gratitude for what was given us—a rich talent, brightly displayed, to an
enduring effect. The testimony of that dying youth is one of thousands from those who have known James Agee as readers, as men
and women grappling with the moral issues of our world and trying
to figure out what truly matters, as against what comes and goes, the
silly, stupid, and all too flashy diversions that tempt many of us, no
matter the region or the neighborhood, to betray ourselves.

Flannery O'Connor

For more than thirty years, my wife, Jane (a high school English teacher), and I kept company with Flannery O'Connor's fictional characters—not to mention the author herself—as she is revealed to us through her essays (collected as *Mystery and Manners*) and her letters (collected as *The Habit of Being*). Each year at Harvard, I brought her voice and vision, her wonderfully drawn characters to the attention of my students (medical students and undergraduate students, and yes, business students), and quickly we responded to the provocative ironies and the edifying paradoxes she poses for her readers. As one medical student told me, "You're not quite the same after you've finished with her." He stopped and took note of the way he had just spoken: he had left out the penultimate word "reading" and in so doing, he had spoken rather more suggestively than he had perhaps intended. Then he decided to be playful with what he had said, with what he would say: "Actually, I could put it this way—you're not quite the same after she's finished with you!"

I thought at the time, and still do, that Flannery O'Connor would have loved that remark. She had such an eye for human complexity; she could fit that complexity nevertheless into the plain, ordinary, blunt idiom of everyday life. Moreover, she was unashamedly assertive, if not truculent, in certain important respects. And yes, she did want us all to be done with a lot of peculiar nonsense that has been touted in this century as a kind of breakthrough knowledge, even wisdom. She also wanted to make clear her impatience, her annoyance even, with those of us who are eternally gullible, or so it seems, ready to worship new idols even before the old ones have lost their grip on us. So that medical student was right to more than hint at the powerfully insistent side of O'Connor's voice which was a determination, I often think, to grab ahold ("aholt"!) of us late twentieth-century readers, and give us more than a run for our money. It was her hope, I suspect, that a lot of us would be "finished" after meeting up with, say, Sheppard of "The Lame Shall Enter First," or Mr. Head of "The Artificial Nigger," or Julian of "Everything That Rises Must Converge," or Hulga of "Good Country People." They are all the same person, and Miss O'Connor would be the first to remind us that she had met that person in the mirror, even as she hoped we'd be lucky enough to catch more than a glimpse of ourselves through whatever self-reflection those relentlessly incisive stories might prompt in us.

Even in the early 1960s, O'Connor's idiosyncratic moral imagination had worked its way into the lives of many of us; so much so that, at the Westminster School in Atlanta, where my wife taught an English class, a janitor who was given to mumbling pieties, shaking his head long and hard when he heard people fight each other with words, and praying on his knees now and then in the midst of his work, was promptly declared by many not a "psychiatric case" (or a medical one) but rather, "a Flannery O'Connor type." My wife always wanted clarification, of course, and the young people she taught weren't usually off the mark. She had taught them O'Connor's stories, and the students had gotten familiar enough with a great writer's vision, close enough to the assumptions and apprehensions that inform a substantial and quite coherent body of work to make certain connections between what someone did that was "odd" in a rather privileged suburban private school (where that

janitor was sui generis) and what O'Connor had some of her characters try to do: take life exceedingly seriously, much to the confusion
and alarm of others.

Milledgeville, Georgia, was the last capital of the Confederacy. Today it is a city of 12,000 people, with a mix of antebellum homes
(still very much a presence and a continuing lure to tourists), an
enormous mental hospital, and a growing number of light indus-
tries. Its real fame, however, is growing for other reasons.

Flannery O'Connor, from Milledgeville, died in early August
1964. She was only thirty-nine years old and had had dissemi-
nated lupus erythematosus since her mid-twenties. The disease had
claimed her father, Edwin O'Connor, who died in 1941 when she
was fifteen.

When she died, Flannery left a legacy of short stories, essays, and
novels. (One of the novels, *Wise Blood*, was developed into a film
directed by John Huston.) Thanks to her friends Sally and Robert
Fitzgerald, another legacy survives—her collected letters, which ex-
tend over the period from June 1948, when she was working on *Wise
Blood*, to July 28, 1964, just six days before her death.

Flannery O'Connor grew up in Savannah, Georgia, and attended
parochial schools there. She lived across the street from the city's
cathedral. In 1941 after her father's death, she was taken to Milledgeville, where she finished high school and attended the Georgia
State College for Women (now Georgia College). The Flannery
O'Connor of the 1940s was a bright, independent person, not especially involved with any particular group or intellectual interest. In
college she majored in the social sciences—something of an irony in
view of her later severe distrust of them. She was adept at drawing
cartoons, deftly executed sketches that reveal a keen, aloof, sardonic
mind. Even at that relatively early point she was able to sense (and to
summon in an art form) the continuing foolishness, hypocrisy, and
pretense from which no era or region can claim immunity.

After she finished college, she found herself stirred to give a verbal rather than a pictorial response to the world she saw around her. Her early writing efforts earned her admission to the writers' workshop Paul Engle ran at the University of Iowa. By the time she graduated from there in 1947, she had already begun to establish herself as a short story writer of considerable originality, power, and, not least, humor. One by one her stories made their appearance in the literary quarterlies as well as in such magazines as *Mademoiselle* and *Harper's Bazaar*. She was accepted at Yaddo, an artists' foundation in Saratoga Springs, New York, and came to know the poet Robert Lowell, the novelist and critic Elizabeth Hardwick, and the poet and translator Robert Fitzgerald. She worked hard on a novel, *Wise Blood*, and in 1949 took up residence in Ridgefield, Connecticut, with Robert and Sally Fitzgerald and their young, growing family. She remained devoted to her mother, Regina (Cline) O'Connor, and to her native South, but she seemed destined to live "up North," near, if not in close contact with, Manhattan's literati.

But in late 1950, illness intervened. Several nights after Sally and Robert Fitzgerald had sent their houseguest south, homeward bound for Christmas, her mother called to tell them that "Flannery was dying of lupus." Sally Fitzgerald continues: "The doctor had minced no words. We were stunned. We communicated regularly with Mrs. O'Connor while she went through this terrible time and the days of uncertainty that followed during Dr. Arthur J. Merrill's tremendous effort to save Flannery's life." The writer was to have fourteen more years, but they were dramatically altered by her lupus.

No doubt about it, we owe to adrenocorticotropic hormone (ACTH) the striking harvest of those years: two novels, some thirty short stories, a collection of brilliant, idiosyncratic, penetrating critical essays, and not least, her recently published letters—*The Habit of Being*. Sally Fitzgerald, a devoted friend of the writer, assembled a large correspondence that becomes, finally, a touching and instructive self-portrait of a novelist.

The physician's success was, of course, purchased at a price. Cortisone exacts its own progressive toll. Reading Flannery's letters, so full of shrewd asides and blunt wisdom, one realizes how much discomfort, pain, and weakness she had to experience as she nevertheless went about her work. It was a stretch of time devoted to approaching closer and closer the essentials of this life—hence the title *The Habit of Being*. (Flannery O'Connor read Maritain closely and knew well his use of the word *habit*. In *Art and Scholasticism* he observes that "habits are interior growths of spontaneous life"—a definition that is a far cry from the view that our behaviorist-oriented society would incline us to have of the efforts we make to bring discipline to our energies.)

Flannery O'Connor wrote stories that were meant to bring us to our senses, to help us sift and sort, to understand what matters truly and what is utterly inconsequential. She was a devout Catholic, although interested in biblical Christianity rather than compliant pietism. She was a Southerner, living in a rural part of the region, but a friend to a number of urban Yankee cosmopolitans. She was, finally, an ailing young woman, living longer and much closer to death than most of us do, whatever our age. But those aspects of her complex life never became an occasion for psychiatric indulgence. That is to say, she had no use for the religious uses to which many have put the social sciences, especially psychoanalytic psychology and psychiatry—the resort to behavioral interpretation or exploration that is meant to serve as a moral substitute for all too many of this age's secularists.

Her letters show her to be willing to say yes or no, willing to approve or condemn, willing to call on the Bible, on a particular moral philosopher or theologian, and yes, on God himself. Her letters, too, show her to be unashamed of tradition—a literary one and a regional one: "To my way of thinking, the only thing that keeps me from being a regional writer is being a Catholic and the only thing that keeps me from being a Catholic writer (in the narrow sense) is being a Southerner." She wrote in a time of unrest and social upheaval. She was repeatedly being urged to "get involved," to speak publicly about racial issues and the Civil Rights struggle, to sign various statements, petitions, and declarations. On the whole, she was guarded and reticent—but not from timidity. She considered herself part of a particular world, the inconsistencies, ironies, paradoxes, confusions, and downright evils that she never shirked evoking in her writing: "The traditional Protestant bodies of the South are evaporating into secularism and respectability and are being replaced on the grass roots level by all sorts of strange sects that bear not much resemblance to traditional Protestantism— Jehovah's Witnesses, snake-handlers, Free Thinking Christians, Independent Prophets, the swindlers, the mad, and sometimes the genuinely inspired." But she was not one to be bullied by those whose self-righteousness or ignorance, however clothed in a moment of virtuous political activity, she could not help perceiving. She loved the South and wanted to see it change, but she knew, as did (in my experience) many of the region's black people, that in the long run it would be the local people themselves—Georgians, Carolinians, Alabamians, and so on—of both races, who would be left to come to better terms with each other. She was, I suppose it can be said, a radical conservative—deeply Christian and hence ever-mindful of Christ's ministry to the poor (most of her fictional characters are poor men and women) but responsive to (and anxious to defend) many aspects of a certain sectional heritage.

Her letters are also, and inadvertently, a chronicle of suffering endured with calm and a knowing dignity. She asks little of her correspondents in the way of sympathy and allows them precious few hints of the pain or physical restriction that is constantly her lot. Only at the very end of her life did she have this to say: "The wolf, I'm afraid, is inside tearing up the place. I've been in the hospital fifty days already this year. At present I'm just home from the hospital and have to stay in bed. I have an electric typewriter and I write a little every day but I'm not allowed to do much." She is, usually, the giver, the one who wants to teach, clarify, reassure, amuse, or offer hospitality. For an increasingly prominent and celebrated writer, she was exceptionally available—quick to reply when a letter or a telephoned or telegrammed request arrived. Guests were welcomed, too—persons from near and far who were drawn to this unusual woman, who may have been sick for years but who seemed a serene, wry, vastly amused observer of her fellow creatures.

At no point did Flannery O'Connor seem inclined to find psychological counsel for her medical predicament. She comes across as utterly uninterested in an examination of the way she was coping with her illness. She would have scorned the extreme self-consciousness of the "awareness movement"—the endless glorification of self that characterizes so much of our contemporary culture. And one can imagine what Flannery (as many of us feel comfortable in calling her, even now as we write of her) would have said about some recent excursions in thanatology. Tell people long enough that hope and prayer and a faith in—a passionate reliance on—God's grace, his promised Good News, are evidence of this or that psychological "mechanism of defense"; tell people they are "using denial" and resorting to "primitive" mental maneuvers; reduce the mind's struggles and yearnings, its long, slouching journey toward Jerusalem to a neurotic fix that needs to be categorized by "stages" and judged as "sick" or "mature"; speak about people and their real-life personal anguish with the stuff of cold, dreary psychiatric jargon—and of course there will be an ironic outcome. Those who once denied us "denial" now give us a denial (voices across the Styx!) that taxes everyone's credulity—in the name of science rather than religion.

No wonder Flannery celebrated mystery and embraced it in the workings of fiction and religion. (As did Hawthorne, she urged that "the task of the novelist is to deepen mystery.") When scientists (let alone social scientists) try to banish all mystery, the result, Flannery knew, would be a mere displacement: the inevitable assertion, as an aspect of our humanity, somehow and somewhere and sometime, of our sense of wonder and awe. Is it presumptuous to suggest *The Habit of Being* as a good text for medical students, physicians, and patients interested in a writer's effort to understand this life?

As Flannery died slowly, and with clear comprehension, she wrote these stunning letters, and they certainly do offer us an example of a remarkable sensibility at work. However strenuous the medical strains provided by a still devastating, puzzling disease, she never yielded her good judgment, her courage, or her deep Christian faith. Her lupus became an occasion for moral reflection and spiritual growth. Her letters remind us what novelists and poets yet have to offer us in medicine—a continuing evocation and celebration of this life's essential nature, not unlike the modest attention we ourselves give to that life, that nature, in the course of our daily medical work.

Dorothea Lange

Dorothea Lange is one of those rare but recurrent figures in a particular American tradition—the artist drawn to the lives of people otherwise unknown, to places seldom visited, to experiences many would prefer left neglected. Such artists have characteristics uniquely their own, not the least of which is a kind of hobo spirit, a companionable feeling for the down and out. Such artists produce texts or pictures that pulse with moral passion, awakening our own connection to the individuals who are their subjects. Such artists go exactly to the moment, exactly to the situation; they create images or works that acquire a measure of universality. The transcendent power of that work, of course, has to do with the observer's artistic gifts.

Lange was an exceptional photographer before—and often a brilliant one after—the Great Depression. Those chaotic years, the vastness of the event, called forth something more in her. Today her images retain their emotional vitality, their faithfulness to the experience, long after the subjects, the circumstance, and the photographer herself have passed from the scene. There are few who possess the intuitive sense necessary for accurate social observation—the identification of the remark, the image, the situation that tells the greater story. There are very few indeed who combine with this capacity the personal vision and developed gifts of the artist. Among Lange's colleagues on the now legendary photography staff of the Farm Security Administration (FSA), there were such artists: Walker Evans and Russell Lee. That fearsome decade of the Thirties also kindled the genius waiting in writers such as John Steinbeck, John Dos Passos, and Clifford Odets. They belong to a lineage that stretches back to Mathew Brady and Walt Whitman and forward to Robert Frank and Jack Kerouac, chroniclers of American manners and mores in the fifties. They are more precious than we might imagine, these artist-observers, in the unfolding experience of our society.

Lange was born in Hoboken, New Jersey, a city William Carlos Williams knew well as a house-visiting physician. At the time of Dorothea Lange's birth, in 1895, Hoboken was, as Williams later described it, a city of "immigrants, from everywhere under the European sun." She was born of such stock, of second-generation German immigrant parents, the first child of Henry and Joan (shortened from Joanna) Nutzhorn, who gave birth to a son, Henry Martin, six years later. Her father was a lawyer, her mother a gentle, beautiful woman who sang in amateur recitals. There was a tradition in the family of the journeyman-artist; three maternal uncles, trained as lithographers in Germany, established a successful business in this country.

Two tragedies tested and shaped the girl. When she was seven she was stricken with polio. The right leg, from the knee down, was impaired. She was called "Limpy" by other children, and for the remainder of her life she would be lame. The handicap haunted her: she accepted but hated it to the end of her life, and at sixty-five she described its significance: "No one who hasn't lived the life of a semi-cripple knows how much that means. I think it was perhaps the most important thing that happened to me. [It] formed me, guided me, instructed me, helped me, and humiliated me. All those things at once. I've never gotten over it and I am aware of the force and power of it."

Many children have been only too willing to find in polio or similar crippling diseases a reason for resignation, if not a withdrawal from the challenges of life. For others there is a redemptive vitality that overwhelms various pains and injuries. In Dorothea, from childhood and throughout life, one gathers, there was a constant effort to make a statement to herself and to others: an impaired gait emphatically does not mean a lagging, curbed life.

When Dorothea was twelve another crisis came upon her: the departure of her father, who walked out, never to return. She never understood why, and could never talk about what happened. There was in her independent nature a habit of closing doors upon past events, of denying the influence of certain experiences and individuals. After the divorce, both daughter and mother adopted Joan's maiden name, Lange. Dorothea kept the secrets of her childhood so well that it was not until after her death that her own husband and children learned that her birth name was Nutzhorn.

Dorothea's mother was left with no money and two small children. She took a job in New York City, as a librarian in a branch of the New York Public Library on the Lower East Side, and enrolled her daughter in nearby Public School 62.

Dorothea and her mother now took the ferry from Hoboken to Manhattan early in the morning, five days a week, into a neighborhood packed with poor people, newly arrived in America. At the time Jacob Riis (*How the Other Half Lives*) and Lewis Hine were both evoking in photographs the vitality, resourcefulness, the desperate circumstances, of lower Manhattan's immigrant life. Suddenly Dorothea was exposed to the likes of Hester Street, the most densely inhabited few blocks in America, crowded with scenes and endless visual excitement. In school, she later recalled, "I was the only Gentile among 3,000 Jews."

If that was an exaggeration, it was an affectionate one. She admired her classmates' ambition, their eagerness to learn. For herself, she was less interested in books than the immediacy of the city's ethnic and cultural life. She absorbed the sights and sounds and smells of lower-class life in turn-of-the-century New York. By herself, each evening, she walked back along Christopher Street to the ferry, wearing what she called her "cloak of invisibility," acquiring by instinct the craft of being the observer unobserved.

Before she was fully grown, Lange had established the distinctive elements of her later working style: a willingness to inquire relentlessly, to move with ease from neighborhood to neighborhood; an interest in the ability of extremely hard-pressed families nevertheless to make do; the stubborn capacity to negotiate through terrible stresses, if not outright disasters; a defiantly rebellious insistence that her own aesthetic and moral interests be affirmed, no matter the prevailing orthodoxies of others, including parents and school officials; and, particularly, a continual attentiveness—an eye that looked hard and remembered.

Another pattern was being set, too, and it was less appealing. After the breakup of her marriage, Joan had set up housekeeping with her mother. Grandmother Sophie was tyrannical, quarrelsome, often erratic—a fine dressmaker and, apparently, a hard drinker. The curious affinity that so often occurs between alternating generations seems to have happened with Dorothea and Sophie. In later life, Lange, too, was a figure of fearsome authority to her children and stepchildren, often lashing out at them over trivial matters and upon occasion—to her dismay—hearing from her own mouth exactly the same harsh, even unjust words she had once suffered from Sophie. Lange was distressed by her intransigence toward her children, but often unsuccessful in controlling it.

When Dorothea reached her late teens, Joan took on a new job as a court investigator assigned to probation cases. Dorothea enrolled in the New York Training School for Teachers on 119th Street. Her attendance was a concession to conformity, to her mother's and grandmother's desire for respectability. She was already certain that her life would be spent with a camera. "My mind made itself up," she later recalled, and could add no other explanation for the decision than: "It just came to me that photography would be a good thing for me to do." She was not yet twenty, and she had never owned a camera.

Lange might shun the classroom, but when she wanted to learn she was tenacious, aggressive, and persuasive. She talked her way into a series of apprenticeships, perhaps the most important with Arnold Genthe, who moved to New York from San Francisco in 1911 and set up a successful portrait studio. In California, Genthe had made portraits of artists, writers, and people of wealth, but he had also documented Chinatown. And when the earthquake of 1906 wrought unparalleled destruction on the Bay Area, Genthe moved amid the rubble. Using a handheld camera, then a relatively new instrument, he created a landmark of American documentary photography.

Among her other teachers were a succession of "loveable old hacks," including one down-at-the-heels itinerant who knocked on the family's door in 1915, showing his wares and offering to take the family's pictures. With his help, she converted a chicken coop into her first darkroom. Only once as a young woman did she take any formal, academic training in photography. In 1917 she attended a course conducted by Clarence White at Columbia University. A private, somewhat elusive man and a gifted teacher (his students included Doris Ulmann and Laura Gilpin), he influenced Lange at a distance. "He knew," she later recalled, "absolutely when something was beautiful." She could not be bothered with the details of White's assignments—but she absorbed a sense of the purity of his artistry.

Her various apprenticeships completed to her satisfaction, Dorothea prepared for the most defiant act of independence of her life to date. She announced to her mother and grandmother that she intended to travel around the world, paying her way as a photographer. The family objected, but Dorothea could not be stopped. In 1918, accompanied by her childhood friend Florence Ahlstrom—a companion in her truancies from school—she set out for San Francisco. Their first day in the city, the two young women had their savings pilfered from their purses, one of the few times Dorothea was ever careless about money.

Almost immediately, she got a job at a photofinishing company where she took orders for picture enlargements and custom-made frames, and occasionally framed the photographs herself. She began to take her own pictures. One of the first people she met, as a customer who walked through the door, was Roi Partridge, the husband of the photographer Imogen Cunningham. They started a friendship that lasted a lifetime, and through the couple she entered into the social life of San Francisco's bohemian set—writers, painters, photographers, and hangers-on. She received a generous offer that allowed her to achieve her goal of setting up a portrait studio and soon attracted prominent and wealthy sitters to her business on Sutter Street. The clientele was largely drawn from families of the wealthy Jewish merchant princes. Years later she would complain of an unfairness: the fame and notoriety of San Francisco's elite had attached to a few mining families, while the Jewish merchants and businessmen truly had created the city's great cultural, artistic, and philanthropic traditions.

It was at Sutter Street, where artists and friends gathered in the evening, that Roi Partridge introduced her to Maynard Dixon. Lange and Dixon were married in the spring of 1920. She was in her mid-twenties, he in his mid-forties. They were a striking couple. She was never a beautiful, perhaps not even a pretty, woman, but her pale, freckled, fine-boned face radiated character and animation. She wore slacks while working, and long, floor-length dresses in the evening, usually with bold, distinctive Indian jewelry. Dixon was a tall, rangy California-born painter and illustrator, respected for his wit, intelligence, and fierce independence. Dixon's bohemianism had a distinctively Western coloration. He knew Arizona and New Mexico well, and he befriended as well as painted his Hopi and Navajo subjects.

Throughout the early Twenties, Dixon and Lange prospered, enjoyed life. His paintings sold well; she was rapidly becoming the best-known portraitist in San Francisco. She had no reputation beyond the city, and she did not consider herself an artist, but she took pride in honest, often charming studies of her clients. The one unhappiness in the family was her inability to respond to the emotional needs of Dixon's daughter by a first marriage. Dorothea applied a certain ferocity to housekeeping: the slightest deviation from her standards enraged her. She didn't understand why, but soon her stepchild was living more in the homes of others, a foster child; and it was a pattern that would be repeated.

Dorothea's first efforts at photographing outside the studio took place in 1922, when she accompanied her husband on a journey through Arizona's high country—small, arid, sparsely inhabited ranch towns, and, of course, the reservations. She took note then of the wretched plight of Indian children—the inadequate, crowded boarding schools they attended, the grim prospects they faced: poverty, joblessness, and, perhaps worst of all, a sense of futility. Theirs was the chronic reservation existence of proud people reduced to ceaseless intimacy with humiliation and defeat. At one stop she took the full-front portrait of a Hopi Indian that became the first powerful image in the Lange opus.

She used her camera on that trip and subsequent ones with no apparent sense of calling, but she was learning. She gradually acquired the knack of moving day after day; of talking with strangers; of absorbing a constantly shifting parade of sights—deserts, canyons, parched rivers, tiny settlements.

The Dixons' first son, Daniel, was born in 1925, and a second, John, in 1928. With the children's arrival, strains emerged in the Dixon marriage. Dorothea found it difficult to accommodate herself to the life of an artist's wife and the mother of small boys. She continued working with her affluent clientele, and placed the boys with friends when she and Dixon went on field trips. When she could not travel, his absences stretched into months. Dixon made little effort to disguise his affairs with other women and, perhaps in retaliation, she, too, took lovers.

As the Twenties advanced, a worsening national economic situation affected them both; they had less money for photographs, murals, and paintings. Lange often found her husband unnerving, a peculiar mix of snob and populist. He had a good deal of contempt for the bourgeoisie—a traditional artist's pose—and he occasionally ridiculed and played practical jokes on her clients, who increasingly provided the main source of their income. In contrast, Dixon responded warmly to the West's working people and its "minorities." Ranchers, cowboys, and Indians, the proud Hispano-Americans of Taos and Truchas and Madrid and Santa Fe in New Mexico—these were the men and women he judged worthy of his time and interest, his affection and his artist's preoccupation. He was deeply affected by the spectacle of a growing national tragedy: millions of moneyless men, women, and children without adequate shelter or food were drifting, dazed, and frightened, while an ever shrinking minority of the wealthy seemed unwilling to recognize the nature and extent of the scandal.

In 1930 and 1931, in part as a desperate bid to save the marriage, Dixon and Lange spent a lot of time in northern New Mexico. Living for months in Taos, they watched the first of the jobless, homeless families moving through the town.

Paul Strand was living in Taos at the time. Lange wondered at the concentration of the man who drove by their adobe each day without looking to right or left. She was intimidated, too shy to introduce herself. She had deeply troubled moments about the direction of her own photography. Two years before, she had returned from a field trip almost in despair about the poor quality of her pictures. Perhaps she was experiencing what the French call a "moment of illumination," a vision summoning her to a different kind of work.

It was not until 1932 that such a vision helped give birth to one of the enduring images of photographic history. Late that year, the Depression had descended upon the country in unalleviated force. The poor and the hungry milled about the streets of San Francisco. Near Lange's studio a wealthy matron known as the "White Angel" had set up a breadline, and the photographer, glancing out the window, watched the cluster of hopeless men waiting for a handout. Worried about the possibility of resentment, even violence, she asked her brother, Martin, who had relocated to the city, to join her as she ventured from the safe confines of the studio with her camera. But the forlorn people in the streets had other things, perhaps only misery, on their minds. She approached the group and started taking pictures of defeated men huddled in their winter coats. Remembering the experience later, she said: "I knew I was looking at something. You know there are moments such as these when time stands still and all you do is hold your breath and hope it will wait for you. . . . You know that you are not taking anything away from anyone: their privacy, their dignity, their wholeness."

In the months that followed, she left her studio at every opportunity and wandered the city's streets. She posted announcements of small, invitation-only showings of her "pictures of people," then "photographs of people"—not the wealthy sitters, but individuals she was discovering in streets, in demonstrations, men and women trailing into the city from blighted states across the union.

In 1934, five of Lange's prints appeared in *Camera Craft*, accompanied by a critical estimate by Willard Van Dyke that remains, perhaps, the best appraisal of her work as she embarked upon the documentary phase of her career.

It was also Van Dyke's exhibition that brought Dorothea together with Paul Taylor, economist from the University of California. His interests, energies, concerns connected so powerfully to her artistic life that one has a hard time imagining Dorothea Lange's career without Taylor—even as her work gave an enormous lift to his aspirations as a socially minded economist, a compassionate activist.

Their first short project together was a study of self-help cooperatives organized to deal with local economic emergencies. In the course of their work together, as he interviewed and gathered data and she photographed the apparently hopeless but valiant efforts of sawmill workers, Lange and Taylor drew close, fell in love. Her marriage to Dixon had entered its final stages: ill, still painting but feeble, nearing sixty, Dixon's one ambition was to return to Taos. Taylor, too, was in the process of obtaining a divorce. The separated couples remained amicable and on December 6, 1935, Taylor and Lange married. In daily life, in work, they would remain virtually inseparable until her death. With Taylor, the union was complete, and together they entered into a period of great accomplishment.

Looking back, the Farm Security Administration (FSA) photography seems like an unlikely, utterly fortunate accident. It emerged in the heady shuffle and reshuffle of government agencies as Franklin D. Roosevelt's New Deal plunged into the task of reviving a shattered economy. Organized under Roy E. Stryker, who also was a relatively unlikely yet happy choice, the FSA Historical Section, as it was formally known, managed to amass more than 250,000 negatives in seven years—an unparalleled chronicle of national change. Far more important, these images were the work of masters, though hardly recognized as such at the time. Walker Evans, Russell Lee, Arthur Rothstein, Ben Shahn, and, of course, Dorothea Lange were among the less than a dozen photographers employed by Stryker, some for only a few months.

After their first expedition together, Taylor managed to have Lange hired as a photographer while he investigated problems of the migrant workers pouring into California. In February 1935, Lange accompanied Taylor and his team on trips to study migrants harvesting in Nipomo and in the Imperial Valley. She had watched him carefully before—his easy, conversational style of coaxing hard data out of the most generalized interview. On the first day, she, too, chatted easily with the destitute migrants, asking about their work, where they came from, their children. Toilets were holes dug in the ground; there was no clean water supply. Work was occasional. Disease and malnutrition showed starkly upon faces of men, women, and children. Lange took pictures, listened, and quickly jotted down the remarks. Taylor was pleased, perhaps surprised. Her field notes figured prominently among the data gathered by his own "trained" assistants from the university, and they were pithy, revealing: "We got blowed out of Oklahoma." "It seems like God has forsaken us back there in Arkansas."

After the trip, Lange helped organize the report, edited and laid out photographs, bound pages. The result was the first appropriation, $20,000, to establish a migrants' camp. It opened in Marysville, California, in October, and set the pattern for a score more. Lange's pictures also won space in newspapers, and the vital editorial support relief efforts needed to overcome—even at the beginning—stormy resistance from the growers' associations.

Taylor's next assignment was with the Federal Emergency Relief Agency (FERA), which had funded the Marysville camp and subsequent settlements. At first, the direct employer was called the Rural Rehabilitation Division, which quickly acquired another bureaucratic niche and name, the Relief Administration, ultimately to be called the Farm Security Administration.

All this occurred just as Taylor and Lange prepared to marry. It was a tumultuous period. The challenges of their work filled them with exhilaration. At home, they had a no less difficult task—merging a family that included her two sons by Dixon and Taylor's three children by his former marriage.

Anxious to be at work, she and Taylor turned their Albuquerque wedding into a working honeymoon. In the afternoon following the ceremony, she went out to photograph. Ambitious expeditions were planned, then canceled for lack of funds. She photographed locally—pea pickers, the devastation of soil erosion.

The early weeks were filled with frustrations for Lange, indecision in Washington. She paid for the first field trips out of her own pocket, and applied for reimbursement. On her first major trip alone in spring 1936, she shot the image that would win a place in newspapers throughout the world and established without doubt the moving, persuasive power of a photograph.

She had been on the road for a month. She had traveled up to fourteen hours a day, photographing, keeping the meticulous records demanded by Washington—of mileage, pennies spent, and exposures made. She had been working over field notes, cleaning and worrying about her equipment. She was returning home on a rainy, cold, miserable March evening. A sign, "PEA-PICKERS CAMP," caught her eye near Nipomo, and she ignored it. Her work was done on that trip, and done well. She drove on for another twenty miles, and, as she later recalled, the question kept recurring in her mind, "Are you going back?" She fought it, even as she wheeled the car around, retraced the twenty miles, drove off the road and into a soggy, forlorn collection of tents. An exhausted mother sitting with her children in a tent caught her eye. Lange spent less than ten minutes with the woman, making five exposures, learning that the crop had frozen, the woman and children were living on vegetables scavenged from the fields, and the few birds the children managed to catch. The mother could not leave; she had sold the tires from her car.

One of those exposures, titled *Migrant Mother*, became the best-known photograph made by Stryker's group, one of the most widely reproduced and exhibited images in history. How reluctantly she had turned around, had headed back to the camp! The picture would never be unequivocally gratifying for Lange. For years she grumbled that it had threatened to make her known as a one-picture photographer.

In the summer of 1936 Taylor and Lange were briefly assigned to Washington. Now their coverage of the dislocations and distress of America's small landholders, its yeomen, its landless rural laborers would acquire the breadth and profundity of the entire national experience. She roamed with camera toward the East, into the South, through the Carolinas, across Mississippi and Alabama.

With or without Taylor, her way of working remained simple, direct, friendly—and honest. She approached a farmhouse, a field, men lounging on the porch of a general store. She struck up conversations easily and to the point: What chores were being performed?

What had the weather been like recently? Were crop prices rising or falling? The answers told her about what people knew—their skills at planting, plowing, cooking. She learned how much money her informants had, what their prospects were. Quickly they grew accustomed to the short, interested woman, perhaps a little outlandish in her slacks, a beret covering her short-cut hair. She asked if she might take pictures and pulled out the two cameras—the Rolleiflex, the 4 x 5 Graflex. She let the children look at the cameras, handle them (something that drove her to fury at home, when her own children touched, sometimes broke her equipment). She seldom shot in doors, seldom used artificial light. But she used everything else she had—including her lameness. No matter that she arrived in a car, worked for the government. The limp showed that she, too, knew the unfairness of life; and she was on their side, wanted to tell their story, wanted to help.

Lange prided herself on never taking a picture of anyone who objected. If she was told not to photograph, she put the cameras away, talked to people, asked again. If they still refused, she drove off. If an individual edged away or hid from the camera, her curiosity was always aroused. Perhaps that was the one, the story, the image. Still, she would not push too hard; she would not override the reluctance of the unwilling. Nor would she aim her lenses at scenes of great emotional stress. Such moments of crisis, she always felt, belonged to the person.

If all was calm in the so-called anthropological field, the relationship between Stryker and Lange was a dizzying mix of quarrels and admiration. He knew well the value of her work to the FSA, to the Administration's relief efforts. A vastly disproportionate share of the requests for illustrations were for the work of Dorothea Lange. Stryker was most anxious to place pictures in such magazines as *Life* and *Look*, rapidly becoming the most widely read publications in the country. Lange's photographs most often interested the editors.

Lange and Stryker also shared an appreciation of the history they chronicled, and, perhaps, were shaping. Each knew that the story of a migrant camp, a displaced tenant farmer, a Texas drought, belonged inextricably to the mosaic of event and change stretching from coast to coast.

Lange's commitment to the division was without qualification. Many years later, she was to say, "Once an FSA guy, always an FSA guy." She liked Stryker, responded with care to his sometimes detailed suggestions, and exchanged ideas for projects. She possessed, as one friend described it, a "pell mell enthusiasm" for her work—once traveling 17,000 grueling miles on an assignment.

Against this background, though, she and Stryker headed toward a serious rift. They might have esteemed each other, but each was opinionated and disagreeable when crossed. Her letters abound with complaints and demands. When advances and back pay were not forthcoming on time, she spent her own money on equipment, supplies, water and electricity, assistants, making Stryker—who was himself battling penny by penny for his division—feel guilty. They argued and he often found her presence in Washington disruptive—even paralyzing.

The crucial argument throughout her tenure with FSA was over possession of negatives. In her letters she constantly pleaded to keep them in California, where she could work on them, supervise printing and selection. He sympathized. The greater need, though, was in Washington, he retorted—the center through which requests from all over the nation passed.

Still, she resisted, and her stubbornness hints at an underlying insecurity—beyond the understandable desire of any photographer to keep possession of negatives. Lange was never a brilliant, perhaps not even a good, technician. She requested, sometimes with success, that her friend Ansel Adams be allowed to develop negatives, make prints. It was a wise choice. He is both a master and innovator of technique. Lange viewed the darkroom with terror, knew the labor required to upgrade her sometimes poorly exposed negatives to good prints. She knew she possessed an eye for reading a negative, for understanding its possibilities. Even more, she knew where the compelling emotional resonance of the print lay.

Stryker tried to compromise by sending her all the negatives she requested, with the provision she return them after the prints were made—a provision Lange always procrastinated about fulfilling. Stryker later recalled, "We practically had to send the sheriff to get them back for the files."

Such quarrels began to erode the Stryker-Lange relationship, more seriously, perhaps, than she knew. In 1938 and 1939 she was on and off the official payroll: sometimes on a per diem basis, sometimes paid by negative—three dollars for each accepted! Stryker's fury reached a peak, however, when he learned that she had hired Ansel Adams to print and mount several pictures—from negatives he had lent back—for a show at the Museum of Modern Art in New York. He was even more enraged that she had hired an expert retoucher to correct flaws on the negatives, including that of *Migrant Mother*. Stryker constantly watchdogged his photographers to make sure they didn't get trapped in "art"—didn't succumb to the "preciousness" of it. He wanted pictures that told the story. There was no objection at FSA to posed photographs, but he was adamant about the purity of negatives.

Lange explained, tried to smooth things over, to no avail. Late in 1939 she was informed, rather curtly, that her employment by FSA would be officially and finally terminated at the beginning of 1940.

For years bitterness lingered between Stryker and Lange. Ultimately, the shared experiences, the remembrance of better times, led them back to a warmer, easier friendship. Still, even in the midst of his anger at Lange, Stryker retained a sense of fair play; he continued to dispatch to Lange and Taylor the negatives for their book *An American Exodus*, which was published in 1939.

Though it found a favorable critical audience, *An American Exodus* was virtually ignored by a public caught up in a different national mood. The war had been unleashed in Europe; America was rearming. Employment increased, at first slowly, then explosively. The historic period that Taylor and Lange had so profoundly conveyed was swept from the nation's mind by the new, even greater drama of a world at war.

Dorothea Lange's accomplishments during those five short years with the FSA are so evident today, so much a part of our national consciousness of the era, that we may well lose sight of how original her contribution was. Her photographs marshaled public sympathy for a necessary relief program. Her photographs persuaded a reluctant Congressional committee to vote funds for that program. Those photographs were part of what is called the documentary tradition. Lange did not need such terms, though; she simply wanted to see and hear, to render and evoke, to transmit, arouse, and record. Yet documentary work, whether visual or written, skirts dangerous edges of misunderstanding and misuse. Always there is the question of motive, of purpose. What were Lange and Taylor really trying to do? What were their aims? The most direct answer is: they were trying to create social and political change. Such a goal, of course, aroused strong criticism from unanticipated, as well as expected, quarters.

When my wife and I talked with Taylor (he was well over eighty) in the Berkeley home he shared for so long with Dorothea Lange, he could still remember the response of any number of his fellow social scientists to the collaborative work he did with his wife. Photographs are "irrelevant," or worse, "subjective," even "inflammatory," he was told. The proper perspective is dispassionate, detached analysis— as opposed to polemical statement, propaganda. Nor would Dorothea Lange be allowed to pursue her intellectual and moral instincts, her particular inclinations as an artist, without a similar kind of reaction from certain colleagues—art demeaned, art as an instrument of indoctrination, of partisan ideological persuasion.

Not all photographers (and not necessarily out of selfishness or heartless indifference) liked the idea of their colleagues spending time and federal money in a constant search for only one side of American life—the "human erosion" Dorothea Lange and Paul Taylor mention in *An American Exodus*. But the book is explicitly meant to be a "record" of that erosion, and by inference, a call for action. The intention, as a work of social science, is unmistakably on the table—to show the waste, the cheapness and meanness of life in the South, in the central states, in our West. Lange and Taylor offered a predominantly visual kind of social geography.

Certainly *An American Exodus* is more than a tale of woe. Some of the photographs show desolation; show a collapsing agricultural order; show perplexity or a contained but unmistakable resentment. But even those black-and-white representations of human reality turn out to be—just that: inescapably ambiguous, in keeping with the strange contradictions of this life.

The problem of preconception, of intent, is paramount to the worker. When my wife and I started going from home to home in Louisiana, Mississippi, Alabama, and Georgia in the late 1950s and early 1960s, an issue rose between us about my point of view. I was a child psychiatrist, I was undergoing psychoanalysis and was beginning psychoanalytic training, and my job was to find out what the serious stress of school desegregation did to the minds of the children and families caught up in the continuing turmoil. We worked conscientiously at that for awhile, but after a month or so my wife became annoyed with me as I pointed out a "denial" here, a "reaction-formation" there. She eventually told me something that I would never forget: "You are always *characterizing* the people we see! Why don't you let them *be*? Why don't you pay attention to each person in each family we visit, and stop trying to lump them together—first one way, then another!" Why not try to get to the heart of the matter in one home, then another—and let the "defense mechanisms" and the "attitudes" and the answers to specific questions take care of themselves?

Even if I hadn't been thereby brought back to sanity, I think I would have had to stop and think again about what I was trying to do in the South, because I was gradually becoming overwhelmed by an astonishing variation in thought and feeling, in opinion and sentiment, in asserted loyalties or preferences, and in asserted dislikes or outright antagonisms. And not only among the black families we'd set out to get to know, but the white people who were, virtually, carrying on a war (certainly with respect to their emotions) against the federal government.

One day we spent a couple of hours with a white New Orleans fireman and his family, and I put each person through a few episodes of questioning, accepted politely and patiently by them. On the way home, I catalogued blind spots and worse. Suddenly, my wife brought me up short: "How many people in this world, including both of us, could survive the kind of scrutiny you give these people? You point out all these things about them. But what if you went into some home in Wellesley, Massachusetts, or Lincoln or Concord, Massachusetts, or yes, Cambridge, Massachusetts, near Harvard Square, and stayed there long enough, and were allowed to ask your questions? How many well-to-do people up there would even put up with it? And if you were given reasonably honest answers, not clever evasions, then wouldn't you come up with some similar evidence—people with their own, distinct ways of putting things, their own choices to make, and people who had their own kind of prejudices, narrowness, and even ignorance?"

Eventually all social investigators must confront these questions, if they are to perform their tasks with any level of competence, much less imagination and skill. Lange deftly solved the problem of intellectual predisposition and prejudice. She knew the literature of her subject matter—the government investigations, the political speeches, the regional histories, the economic and social surveys. Her habit was always to research after the fact, after the photographic expedition. She spoke often of the need for blankness, the value of the receptive eye in photography. First came the image, then the research that interlocked the intricate features of the history she was recording. Obviously this is the closest anyone can approach to objectivity. Less obvious is the rarity of such practice, the passion for comprehensive understanding, particularly among photographers who often sacrifice breadth and profundity, in the name of visual purity.

An even greater problem for those who do documentary work exists on the ethical level: the very nature of the work risks injustice. But that does not mean the work is evil or should not be attempted. When the critic Susan Sontag in *On Photography* uses words such as "aggression," "imperial," and "capture"; and when she talks about photography as a "tool of power"; and when she declares that photographs enable people to take "possession" of the past, of space, of experience—she is echoing a Victorian scrupulosity which is, of course, inadequate. In whose name, in what name, are her moral misgivings and outright condemnations handed down? Whether photographer, writer, or filmmaker, anyone who presumes to examine the lives of others must continually subject himself or herself to self-scrutiny, lest the pitfalls Sontag so narrowly ascribes to photography cloud the very goals he or she wishes to achieve.

My wife and I struggled with the issue of "balanced" reporting for many years. I never had a chance to discuss that equation with Dorothea Lange, but I did meet W. Eugene Smith, who spent his life photographing the needy from Haiti to Japan. He spoke eloquently on behalf of victims who need a voice, who need to be seen as witnesses to their suffering: "I believe the people I'm with know what I'm trying to do and want me to go ahead," he once told me. I wondered, however, whether there isn't some room for misunderstanding—for the observer to assume a commonality of analysis and purpose in his or her own interests.

The ultimate, eternally worrisome question to be raised is this: to what extent does even the finest, most rigorous documentary effort serve the lie more than the truth?

Dorothea Lange seldom raised the issue. Toward the end of her life, she invariably, and accurately, referred to photography as a "medium." She meant that word in its exact sense—a means of

conveying something. To our great disadvantage we of this generation have yielded to Marshall McLuhan's banality that "the medium
is the message." Stryker, Lange, and the other FSA photographers
had another purpose in mind. They were obsessed with the realities of their time: they confronted not a "subject," an "example," or a
"respondant"—they confronted circumstances and situations; they
confronted "fellow human beings." They moved in the realm not of
the abstract, but of the concrete—like William Carlos Williams,
saying what he had to say not through a discussion of ideas, but "in
things." In so doing those photographers defied even their employer,
the Farm Security Administration.

For the best of reasons, the FSA wanted Lange's help in educating a nation—teaching its citizen voters what was wrong, sorely
wrong, with an economy, by showing them how much wretched-
ness had suddenly come upon an advanced industrial nation. Yet her
American people, her American land, her barns and stores and road
scenes attest to a vitality, a perseverance, a willfulness; one can even
find "beauty" in all that injury and perplexity—strong, handsome
faces, vigorous bodies, attractive buildings, a grace and grandeur to
the countryside, even its ailing parts. An artist has asserted herself,
it can be said—no matter a strong interest in polemical statement,
in argumentative portrayal. In her later, international work the same
tension persists: Lange as the pained observer, herself reasonably
well off, yet terribly cognizant of, responsive to the difficult situation of so many others; yet, Lange as the visual observer, the person
whose sensibilities are extremely broad, and whose representational
faculties are awake, energetic, stubborn, and refined. In Ireland, in
Nepal, in Egypt, in Korea she saw extreme poverty. She also saw
objects to admire; scenes to record in all their striking charm or
symmetry; faces of men, women, and children whose dignity, whose
inviting loveliness simply could not be denied or overlooked.

In 1941 Lange, Taylor, and their children moved into a new home,
the first they had owned. It was an open redwood-and-glass struc-

ture flooded with light, set on a tree- and plant-covered hill. Here, they would live for the rest of their lives. Here, she created an atmosphere of order and beauty, with simple, Shaker-like furniture, with bowls, pottery, and basketry from the regions where she had worked.

In 1945, Lange was asked by the State Department to photograph the San Francisco conference that established the United Nations. She accepted, with misgivings. Her stomach was always delicate, a continuing hindrance even during the halcyon Thirties when she traveled tens of thousands of miles. The symptoms were becoming more severe. Ignoring her doctor's advice, she went ahead with the UN assignment. Shortly afterward, she was seized with violent pain and hospitalized. For the next eight years, severe ulcers kept her from attempting any camera work away from home, and on several occasions nearly killed her.

As a result, Lange did, finally, get to stay with her family in the redwood house. The longing had always been there, the guilt about allowing her children to be raised by friends and relatives had never ceased. The internal bleeding may have had at least some origin in the conflict between work and home. Now, and for the rest of her life, Lange would find her joy, her interests, and indeed some of her final best images in the family, the setting of the home, the simple objects in her kitchen and studio.

Her final project, the one that now meant the most to her, was "To a Cabin," a photographic study of her children and their children at the beach cottage at Steep Ravine. She turned from that study, reluctantly abandoned it, when the Museum of Modern Art's curator of photography, John Szarkowski, informed her—didn't ask; he knew she would resist—that he planned a major retrospective exhibition of her work. Only a half dozen photographers had ever been so honored.

The final two years of Lange's life were devoted to a review of her lifetime's work. From tens of thousands of negatives she and Szarkowski selected the 200 prints to be exhibited; painstakingly they arranged, balanced, and harmonized the images, panel by panel. Curator and photographer worked well together; they knew when to admire one another and when to argue. She would plead for pictures that told a story she liked; he would suggest the picture that had the greatest impact as an image—the superior picture.

She worked and worked hard—at times exhausted after only twenty minutes of effort. She was afraid—not of the illness, not of death. She was confronting a lifetime of work, and worried about its worth. But, as she told an interviewer making a film of her, "When you get to the point I'm at, there's no point to anything *but* risks." On the very day she died, October 11, 1965, Dorothea Lange was still the documentary field-worker—trying to wrest the truth for others to see. Her retrospective exhibition opened three months after her death.

It is fitting in connection with Lange's work to reflect on William Carlos Williams and Walt Whitman, even on those decidedly aristocratic, wonderfully astute observers of America, Alexis de Tocqueville and Henry James. The last of these may have summarized it all—what any of us who try to do "documentary studies" can only hope to do with a small quota of his brilliantly penetrating success: "The manners, the manners," his terse mandate of what must be seen, what must be set down for others to see. Whitman was more celebratory, less dispassionate. Williams was a fiery enthusiast, a mordant critic, if not a vigorous combatant. The French visitor de Tocqueville was less literary than James, more systematic in his elegant, nineteenth-century prophesy of America's coming history. Lange reveals elements of all those observers in her work. In the Jamesian tradition, she can concentrate on the distinctive appearance of a woman's neck, on the complementary splendor of two shoes, on the extended power of a particular barn's sloping roof. She can roam America, follow its various roads, large and small, marvel at the variety and robustness of our people—in the tradition of Whitman: a gentle and loving, but also a tough, willful, and resourceful traveler, determined to return home with productive, inspiring memories. She can shake her fists—as Williams used to do—at the stupidity of so many, the needless injuries to people who deserve better; and like him, she can summon a redemptive, celebratory music in response to what she has seen others experience, and through them, herself experienced. She can even be the careful analytic student de Tocqueville was—those hands she gives us, those tools, those clothes, those signs; in sum, those physical aspects of existence that reveal so much about a given people's aspirations and difficulties.

Dorothea Lange was finally another restless visionary artist, using film to make the point novelists and poets and painters and photographers and sculptors all keep trying to make: I am here; I hear and see; I will take what my senses offer my brain and with all my might offer others something they can see or hear, and doing so, be informed, be startled, be moved to awe and wonder, be entertained, be rescued from the banality, the dreary silliness this world, inevitably, presses upon us. She failed at times, failed personally, as she herself acknowledged, when she discussed the many leaves of absence from her home, her young children; failed artistically, when she lapsed into the photographer's version of coyness, rhetorical overstatement, repetitive posturing. But she succeeded repeatedly—gave us our rock-bottom selves: a clear and trenchant portrait of any number of this earth's twentieth-century people.

Bruce Springsteen

In the twelfth and thirteenth centuries, certain poets moved across territory that is now southern France, northern Spain, and northern Italy; from town to town those poets spoke of life as it then was being lived, and of social and political matters of significance. Often the poets were accompanied by individuals who made music of the poetry, and then sang the words before the crowds that quickly, eagerly gathered. The poets were known as troubadours, and the apprentice musicians as jogleours. Sometimes the two attracted more than passing interest and attention; they became eagerly awaited catalysts of public discussion and reflection.

There were about four hundred troubadours in all, and by the thirteenth century they were gone, their compelling artistic originality and public presence having threatened Church and State alike. Once, speaking of their brief time in Western Europe's social and thinking and singing life, William Carlos Williams engaged in what he called "dreaming and yearning" with these words: "If we had troubadours, American troubadours, singing their poems to us (in person, not on some movie screen or 'home television set'), maybe we'd be stopped still for a bit, so we could think about where we're heading, and where we might prefer to be headed."

Williams himself was one such American troubadour; he often spoke of the poet in him as a part of his mind and heart that ached to sing—as (he would remind his listeners) one of America's greatest poets, Walt Whitman, did when he wrote "I Hear America Singing," a poem that celebrates "the varied carols" the writer could hear: the workers of a fast-growing nation—the mechanics, the carpenters, the masons who build it, the mothers and wives and plowboys and boatmen who sing away with others; an American chorus that is assembled by a poet become his orchestra's conductor. Often Dr. Williams called himself a "New Jersey boy": he was born in New Jersey; he lived there throughout his life of almost eighty years, and he died there. He knew the state well, having visited patients in various towns and cities; it was his "home state," he often remarked, and he loved the "nickname," he called it, of the Garden State. "Lots of growing around here," he once said, and then he ranged widely, touting names and accomplishments: "We've had singers from Whitman, who sang through his writing, up to this Sinatra fellow, who's doing right well with his voice."

Dr. Williams was under ten when Walt Whitman, a resident of Camden, New Jersey, died in 1892. Williams called Whitman a "New Jersey boy, finally"—true enough; and "the Doc," as many called Williams with both respect and familiarity, steeped himself quietly in some of Whitman's poems, most especially "I Hear America Singing" and two "To the States" poems he called them; "To the States" is tersely theoretical, and "On Journeys Through the States," longer, salutes the ever-growing diversity of our nation's sweeping breadth.

Were Dr. Williams alive today, he'd no doubt be calling another American singer a "New Jersey boy." Bruce Springsteen was born in Freehold (what Williams would have done with that town's name!) in 1949, and so was fourteen when Williams died in 1963; and there it is, a line from the early 1880s to the early 1960s—the proverbial fourscore, encompassing parts of the lives of three New Jersey boys:

Whitman's toward his life's end, Williams's all through his life, and Springsteen's, of course, still very much with us. In a sense, the "boy" in between foresaw the boy who would follow him.

All three of those Americans were intent on responding to a nation's people—catching alive their voices and offering them to those who read, those who listen. The songs Springsteen presents to his audience are all his in the thinking, the writing. His lyrics speak of his life's awareness, the sights he's witnessed, the sounds (the pleas, the cries, the shouts) he has heard his fellow citizens express, and has heard within himself as he goes about being a resident, still, of New Jersey: a husband (of Patti Scialfa, a singer), a father (of their three children, two sons and a daughter), and a member (with his wife) of a music-making community. The E Street Band, which periodically goes on tour, becomes for city after city a rallying ground for music sung, played, heard, but also for music that stirs listeners to look within deeply and, in the words of one listener, "to hear the music my own mind is making and playing while I try to make a life, play with life, get on top of it." That comment tells a lot about what Dr. Williams would have celebrated about Bruce Springsteen—his willingness (and ability) to convey music to others through his voice, to work with others who make music through musical instruments (all of them becoming a band and one of them becoming its vocalist), and his further, extraordinary initiative: the writing of personal lyrics which turn music making into an occasion of shared observation and reflection—stirred by those doing that work on a stage, or in a studio, and then sent back in kind by listeners who have paid attention, at a concert or at home, and who pay further inner regard as they go about their ruminating lives.

There are, of course, many ways that we are moved to thought— by others with whom we live and work, by those we meet in the course of going about our daily lives, and not least, by others we meet (see or hear) when we go to the movies, watch the television screens in our homes, hear the radios at home, or in our cars, or through the sets we carry with us.

For a New Jersey physician and poet, the singer was a messenger, *there* for the listeners in the way we human beings can often be: the bearer of tidings, of news good and bad, of happy possible prospects, or of the melancholy side of things that it is our mortal destiny to understand as we turn the many corners in the travels we take through space and time. Dr. Williams was quick to bring in others—the beloved members of his family, his friends and neighbors, his fellow writers, and not least, those who once lived and struggled with words and are now "gone in body but here in mind and spirit," he'd say during some of his candid talks about his work. He spoke of others apart from writers—of Dorothea Lange and Frank Sinatra; he also spoke of the Hoboken that was the birthplace of those two, and of its people, fellow tillers of the New Jersey soil, its harvest of life, amidst its places of hurt, suffering, death—the hospitals and clinics and cemeteries to be found in Hoboken and elsewhere across that state and the other forty-nine, which in sum give us today's America. "Go to Hoboken if you want to know that guy Sinatra, if you want to know Dorothea Lange," he once said—he was wandering through memories and wondering about how it would be decades ahead, after his death, for the New Jersey people he knew so well. Changes aplenty he knew were in store for the fast-changing American scenes to be observed in various regions of a nation that extends across a continent. Those changes would enable us to travel further and know more about each other through the developing technology he could only imagine, without being able to spell out specifically its characteristics.

Like so many intuitive and knowing people, he knew how to get at what would always matter. "You never do know when and where a new traveling companion will show up for you—*there* with you, out of a book you bumped into, or a picture that hit your eyes and stayed a long time in the back of your head, or a song that took you over: the singer became your pal, your guide—even, for a few minutes, your inspiring teacher who got you thinking like never before."

Those words were spoken late in 1955, and less than a decade later the one who offered them to another person had left us all. In 1988, twenty-five years after Dr. Williams departed this life, I sat remembering him as I heard a singer tell us, hearing him, that a lot was happening still in the New Jersey a poet (and novelist and essayist) had very much wanted us to get to know. The singer was brought to my attention by my sons, who kept on telling me that the one singing was kin of sorts to that New Jersey "Doc" whom they knew from the words in books, or through certain letters held dearly in the house, or by the references their parents on occasion made, their faces showing the wistful recollection that the past, once summoned, can prompt. The selling point: This singer was from New Jersey, was born and bred there, went to school there, started making music there, and was briefly (at the age of twenty-two) called "the Doc" in a group known as Dr. Zoom and the Sonic Boom. With that name offered, I was convinced that a prank was under way. I was ignorant but interested, and soon thereafter began to listen harder to the music that resounded through their rooms and any others their mother and I hadn't managed to shut off courtesy of doors. With my interest growing, silence in part of the house yielded to music become, only briefly (thank God!), widespread, triumphant: the Boss became the Boss of all the house's hearing inhabitants.

Now I knew some of the Boss's songs, and now I began paying attention to mention of him among the young people in my classes and among those parents and children I was getting to know as part of my effort to learn the ways various kinds of American families came to terms with their working and home lives. All this I kept putting on the record in my writing, while wondering what to make of these "Springsteen echoes," as I dubbed them, in my notes. As my sons left for college, the Boss's world began to fade from our house, though not from my life. For instance, a young law school student told me of a childhood memory: He is standing in a shower as a young boy, his father nearby—and Bruce Springsteen is singing away, his voice coming out of a nearby electronic disc-playing gadget. The music is more than holding its own against the splashing water, and the parent is clearly delighted to be ridding himself of the day's sweat and grime, while his son follows suit with less savvy or reason to be where he is, while Springsteen hails a nation and its hardworking people in homes not unlike this modest but comfortable one wherein a father and son are enjoying their time together and with their guest, whose upbeat, vigorous voice does well by the stories he keeps relaying. Those stories are his own, not those of an anonymous or far-off composer or lyricist who never actually sings the songs he puts together. "That's three people doing what the Boss does on his own," one of my sons let me know—lest I be unaware of the division of labor that often takes place in the world of music, as against Springsteen's extraordinary solo initiative, years in the creative making.

Once, on my way to visit Rutherford, New Jersey, where Dr. Williams had been born and spent a good part of his life, I found that one of my sons had put a Springsteen tape on the seat next to mine, and so I picked up *Darkness on the Edge of Town* and began hearing the songs as I drove across Massachusetts, Connecticut, New York—and then the "big crossover," as Doc Williams used to call it, referring to the bridge (or tunnel) that carries you into New Jersey. By then I'd met Springsteen as millions of others had—on the covers of *Time* and *Newsweek* in 1975. He had "climbed to the top," a fellow physician had remarked. At that time, we were working with children in a ghetto, visiting them in their homes, but several of us had been invited to be connected to universities, to work (and try to heal and teach) in that world "across town, across the tracks," as the saying goes, and this medical colleague was warning us (himself included) about the ultimate, possibly moral consequences of such a move. He wanted to be honorably skeptical—and at one point he summoned Bruce Springsteen as a witness, if not example: "You rise and rise, and then you're in danger of selling out: you make a lot of dough for yourself and those around you—but what happens to your ideals, the values that pressed you to do what you once did? This guy [Springsteen] was once a fighting kid—the kind who would be sent to see us: rebellious, having trouble at school, having a 'problem with authority,' all the shrink talk you folks and I are supposed to use when writing in those hospital charts. He was an outsider, taking potshots at stuffy, full-of-themselves insiders; but then he became what he is now: a big-deal success story, with a big payoff, the reward for going only so far, but no further, in zeroing in on the downside of capitalism. You start out a populist, singing of the downtrodden, and you end up being careful enough when you sing not to offend the principalities and powers—that's his story, and that is becoming ours!"

I had tape-recorded that relentlessly tough statement at my friend's request. I was using my tape recorder all the time with the families I was visiting, and my friend wanted to be heard and heard, his remarks available to me, and our mutual friends, working colleagues, should we desire to go back to them. He was emphatically not being self-righteous (an occupational hazard, alas, for all who have the moralist in them); rather, he was worried about where people like us were headed and, more broadly, where an increasingly powerful and rich America was headed—with, I realize now in retrospect, Vietnam haunting us. All through that drive to visit the home of a hero of mine, to talk with his family and friends, I played Bruce Springsteen's music but remembered what our friend had told us about an admired singer who kept challenging, if not provoking, his audience even as he brought them closer to the exciting warmth of love—what novelists have done for centuries: through stories of love, the reader is warmed, encouraged to take of the same cup whose qualities are being contagiously, affectingly described. It is one thing, my friend had insisted, to be turned on by love songs; it's another to be turned on by songs about others, their trials and tribulations; but if you end up "turned off" politically, and go back to being compliant all over the place, with no fire of anger at the social and political wrongs, then: "You've let yourself be silenced, conned—your conscience is shut down. And that's where the singer Springsteen and the rest of us are in this together, this cop-out."

By the time I'd reached Rutherford, the sense of moral ambigu-
ity, the feeling of anguish which my friend had hoped to get going in
us had cooled down. There are plenty of alternative ways of thinking
available under such circumstances, and they were well in control of
my mind as I neared Dr. Williams's home. When there, with the
memory of him, I soon realized how heavy a burden of illness he'd
daily carried as he tried his best, at the end of his life, to keep afloat,
keep up with life's daily rhythms, though confined to his home and
not up and about. The memory of many brief, pleasant visits stayed
with me—however, the cloud of his falling health seemed to return,
darkening my mood. On the way back, Springsteen's songs filled
the car's air and hit my head hard. I thought of the two of them,
those New Jersey boys, I was calling them in my mind, the Doc
and the Boss. Hence, a few weeks later, my thoughts still circling
and circling, the following poem:

NEW JERSEY BOYS

TO W. C. W.

You two gardeners,
Both you bards, Bill and Bruce,
The Doc and the Boss,
Who never wanted to skip
The heartbeat of home—
Stay there, your choice·
Claiming the spread below the Hudson.
No bridge or tunnel worked for you,
The local turf gave you plenty to do—
Soil to pick up with bare hands;
Bring sun to warm it up,
Let drafts of air turn it on,
See its excitement grow.
Let the twin tallest buildings in the world
Signal their dough to the torch-lady nearby;

Lots of folks who scare up the blinds in the morning
Are spared the hangout—the hang-ups—of the big shots.
You two gardeners and your trips to the city:
"The Lonely Street" was followed
Decades later by "Racing in the Street."
Each of you made the trek:
So many hustles to see,
All the colors and sounds, the words and deals,
Cards to be dealt, decks stacked,
A throw of the dice daily:
Plain life and crying shame deaths,
None of the Eros and Thanatos stuff
You hear in abstract elsewheres.
"Hey," you both pleaded,
"No starch in the shirts."

Both you gardeners raked:
Sweat all day and kiss
When you're lucky to find the lips.
No tax credits, just the tax itself, all the time,
Hoping for a break, a day off
Now and then, and the kids, they might do better,
Though it's always tough in Paterson,
And lots of times Nebraska is no picnic.

You guys, the gardener Walt's kin,
Whose beard we all know
(Its secrets keep a growth industry busy—
Leafing through his grass)
You two, from Ridge Road and E Street,
Each out to put it on the line, put them there:
Ordinary ones, whose lumps pollsters rush
To palpate only now and then.
You two are permanent guests,

Listening and showing your love in words, in notes
Two bards, Bill and Bruce,
The Doc and the Boss: America—
Love it or leave it to you both to know,
And give back to us, maybe our only chance.

Dr. Williams often spoke of "traveling with others through time" as well as space—his way of getting at a comradeship of ideas and ways of thinking about life and, too, giving expression to what he deemed important through poems, plays, essays, stories. So also with a poet who sings the words he has assembled; not only are Springsteen and Williams geographically kin but both are poets of ordinary American people, who are trying to make do in their own lives—sometimes falling down, but again and again ready and willing to pick themselves up, to keep trucking, as it is said by some young Springsteen fans I know. Springsteen gets his listeners to think about their own lives, even as in various ways they use his words of reflection, heightened in their intensity by his voice sending them forth. So it went too with many of us who gave attention and high regard to Dr. Williams's verse-making (and sometimes fighting) literary life. Speaking to an audience in Chicago in 1955, he referred to the "connections that tie some of us taking the same road"—he was, again, circling around that theme of traveling companionship. It would be for us, his readers, to think of some of those companions—he was so busy trying to keep moving, and anyway, that is what a writer or a singer does: invites (in readers or listeners) considerations, comparisons, connections.

Some of us who do our own traveling, called sociological or anthropological fieldwork, or documentary studies, can only with a certain awe note how carefully and knowingly Springsteen today observes Americans of all sorts and conditions—then tells of what is there, awaiting our awareness, recognition. The traveling observer first, then the singing storyteller, makes us listeners his traveling companions—Americans who have been taken across America by a fellow American, and through his working, writing, singing life they have met other fellow Americans: all of them, that way, belonging to Bruce Springsteen's America, and all of them given plenty to ponder.

Bruce Springsteen writes down his observations, concerns, experiences, ideas, and ideals, then writes songs he sends toward his hearing fellow human beings, fellow American citizens—songs of his nation's, our nation's ups and downs, possibilities and problems, breakthroughs and breakdowns, become all of ours to consider within our day-to-day lives. A writing singer's inwardness eventually becomes the inwardness and the outwardness of so many people, who attend his concerts, buy recordings, turn on radios, and thereafter go back to the heard, the told and sung, as it works its way into, connects with, particular listeners doing their own daily turns of thought, feeling, and speaking. Springsteen sings of and about America, and some of his country's people take in what he says, sings, and make it their very own, pro or con—his feelings, assertions, avowals, descriptions, admonitions: a nation addressed lyrically, gravely admired, loved, admonished, portrayed, warts and all.

Bruce Springsteen's America becomes, in sum, all of us, travelers in time: ever so many personal variations on one singer's poetry put to music, his feelings and themes, given voice, then heard, then taken to heart far and away, abroad a country's sweep.

III.

Lives of Moral Passion

Simone Weil

Perry Miller introduced Simone Weil to us in his class during the spring of 1950. The course he taught, "Classics of the Christian Tradition," was part of the new (post–World War II) General Education Program at Harvard College. Miller was a historian for whom the religious life of the New England Puritans was of commanding importance. But he was far from provincial: he had a particular passion for Kierkegaard's cranky, morally compelling essays, which were gradually being translated into English during the late 1940s and early 1950s; and another hero of sorts to him was Dietrich Bonhoeffer, whose personal courage in the face of Nazi absolute rule, evoked by an especially compelling teacher, kept us all in perplexed awe as we contemplated what makes for decency in extremis.

Not that we could dash to the Harvard Coop in those days and buy our paperback copies of *Gravity and Grace*, or *The Need for Roots* or *Waiting for God*, or the *Letters and Papers From Prison* and *The Cost of Discipleship*, books I now keep near, use in a course I teach, and still find intimidating to read—and doubly intimidating in their very availability, as if, in their sum, they offer ample evidence that there is nothing that the Western haute bourgeoisie (the branch of it known as the "intelligentsia") can't take for granted, dip into now and then, even on one or another rainy day feel intensely drawn to, though not in such a fashion as to jeopardize a quite comfortable life. Back then there was, mostly, Perry Miller's voice, telling us about Bonhoeffer and Weil, a pair of figures yet to become legendary and quickly classifiable as extraordinary twentieth-century moralists willing (in different ways) to die for their beliefs. In Paris *La Pesanteur et la grâce* had just been published (1948), followed by *L'Enracinement* (1949). I would read them later, in 1954, while a medical student, and reread them (in English) while doing the pediatric part of my internship.

To this day I wouldn't want to improve upon Perry Miller's presentations of Weil. He connected her, forthrightly and confidently, with Pascal, whose *Pensées* and *Provincial Letters* he had demanded that we read and know in great detail: the scientifically sophisticated, skeptical mind grappling seriously with the matter of faith—and interested in doing so publicly, that is, in a literary gesture which makes others companions or adversaries. He also reminded us that writers such as Kierkegaard, Pascal, and Weil are strong-minded social critics—anxious to connect the Gospel to this life we live, as opposed to emphasizing abstract theological discussion or the virtues of one or another ritualistic orientation. They belonged (he showed us through textual analysis) to an existentialism not yet corrupted by secular, faddish embrace. They were (he would take pleasure in indicating) bold eccentrics—quite willing to be at a remove from reigning "principalities and powers," even those within the particular religious community they both addressed, yet criticized.

When my wife and I went south in 1960 to work with children going through the trials of school desegregations, or youth involved in the civil rights movement, we took certain books with us, an iconography of sorts: Agee's *Let Us Now Praise Famous Men*, some stories by Flannery O'Connor and Eudora Welty, Faulkner's *The Sound and The Fury* and *Light in August*, C. Vann Woodward's *Tom Watson*, and books by Paul Tillich and Reinhold Niebuhr, both of whom had meant a lot to us in the 1950s because of their continuing efforts, in the middle of the twentieth century, to think of what the Christian tradition demands of those who want to be part of it.

I remember a discussion my wife and I had, at the time, about Simone Weil. I was holding in my hand Weil's *La Condition ouvrière*, a paperback published in 1951 by Gallimard, with nuts and bolts ostentatiously pictured on the cover. The message to the person browsing in a bookstore was surely this: you of the intellectual sort (who buy books, and if you're American, read French) might want to read this book (one in a series called "Idées"!) in order to learn about how others, less fortunate, manage to live their lives. Moreover, as the publishers hastened to tell one in the jacket copy, "l'auteur dégage la philosophie et la morale de cette expérience." How could an aspiring psychological and social observer, with the ambition to write about what he would see of a relatively poor or (so-called) "working-class" world fail to say yes to such a book, such an author? My wife, less enthusiastic, wanted us to leave behind not only Weil's books but *all* the books mentioned above: "Let's take nothing but ourselves—a few changes of clothes and that's it; we can always buy a book or two as we go along." I thought at the time she was worried about the problem of space in our beleaguered, faltering station wagon.

We took the books, and when we got a flat tire, halfway down the New Jersey Turnpike, I sure wished we had left them behind. I remember eyeing *The Need For Roots* as we pushed our way through boxes in order to find the tools that would enable us to change tires. Afterwards, merrily headed for the Delaware Bridge and points south, she came to both our minds, Simone Weil and her notions of place, of community, of nationality. My wife mentioned that she had read *The Need For Roots* in a course at Harvard (1958), and found it hard going. She also remembered hearing Weil described as "anorectic." We both dismissed that categorization, yet we were both making a connection in our conversation of a kind that every student, every biographer of that enormously learned and hard-to-figure philosopher and essayist has, in one way or another, found it necessary to make—the relative density of a given writer's narration and the personal difficulties she kept having all through her brief, intense, dramatic life.

Once settled in Louisiana, and later, Georgia, we had little time for those books. But in 1963 I began "seeing" a young civil rights activist who was having personal difficulties and had asked me whether we might informally meet and talk. I was, at the time, working closely with SNCC (the Student Non-Violent Coordinating Committee) and talking informally with many of those who made up its membership, an effort on my part to understand how and why young people became involved in social causes and political action. This student, however, wanted not to talk about his ideas, his beliefs, or the reasons he'd become a committee member of SNCC, but his recent and ongoing troubles with his girlfriend, his disagreements with his father about what career eventually to pursue, and not least, his worrisome physical health, over which I'd heard him fret before we started meeting in a downtown Atlanta cafeteria, once a week, for a more structured and personally involving kind of conversation than had been the case before. Put differently, I no longer asked him the general questions—about background, and family ideas, ideals, convictions—that I'd been putting to youthful activists for several years. Instead, he told me about his worries, his lapses of bad temper, his spells of severe depression, and his feeling at times that he was "old," that life was passing him by, that he would "die young." (Two of his close friends in "the movement" had been seriously hurt in an encounter with Alabama's state police, and so there was an element of "reality" to his unpleasant daydreams or not-so-random concerns, worries, trains of thought.)

One Thursday morning (our "regular time"), he told me of a new symptom: he'd not been able to eat much. He felt dispirited, was not sleeping "all that well," and found himself surprised that instead of eating a bit *more*, as was the case when he'd known low spirits in the past, he now was eating less, much less—to the point that he was losing weight, and others were noticing that fact. (To my mind he'd been, all along, fairly thin.) I was about to pursue that matter, ask him the doctor's usual questions, meant to ascertain how long the "problem" had been going on, whether there were specific foods being shunned, and too, any accompanying symptoms—nausea, vomiting, headaches—and on and on went the mind which had studied hard and long a book titled *Signs and Symptoms*. But before I'd begun my seemingly haphazard inquiry—one of the best teachers at medical school had encouraged us to be gentle, unobtrusive, even willfully "a bit disorganized" so as not to alarm our patients, and quite possibly prompt them to stop talking—the young man took the initiative of changing the subject abruptly by asking me if I'd ever read "any Simone Weil." I nodded, and readied myself for *my* questions, but he wouldn't defer. Which books of hers had I read? What did I think of them? What did I think of *her*—the way she lived her life, including its ending? I wasn't all that sure of what to reply—after, that is, I'd recited a list of books and indicated (what else?) a decided interest in her work. My friend, I began to realize, was more strongly touched than I by what he'd been reading—not only Weil's writing, but what had been by then written about her: Leslie Fiedler's introduction to *Waiting For God*, T.S. Eliot's preface to *The Need For Roots*, the statement addressed to the readers of *Gravity and Grace* by Gustave Thibon, her dear friend, and not least, a valuable biography and critical study by the English philosopher E.W.F. Tomlin.

I remember deciding (how condescending, how patronizing!) that the fellow sitting across the table from me, sipping black coffee and nibbling guardedly some unbuttered toast (his breakfast and lunch both) was somehow "blocked by conflict" or was trying to evade a necessary confrontation with his increasingly serious (I'd decided) "psychopathology." I also remember concluding that I would wait if he seemed to want to wait (noblesse oblige!), and that I would then and there forget about the ostensible purpose of our meeting and continue the discussion of Simone Weil so evidently desired by my friend. After I left him I hastened to a bookstore and ordered the

Tomlin book. When I got home I found myself poking through our books, not stationed in bookcases because we hadn't bought any. We were, then, reading magazines and newspapers, mostly, about what was happening to the South; and so the books we'd brought down seemed to belong in those cartons where they'd been since our arrival a couple of years earlier. It didn't take too much poking for me to come up with the Weil books, though only when I *saw* them did I realize that I had been looking for them.

I mention this incident because in a strange way it got me going, so to speak, on a very intense reading of Simone Weil's work. The student was one of the young heroes of our civil rights movement, one of the finest Southern whites to break with his own personal past and take a stand against segregation. He was also a very devout Christian, and he'd been reading Bonhoeffer, whose *The Cost of Discipleship* had only recently (1961) been published in this country. As we talked on successive meetings about Weil, and then Bonhoeffer, I began to notice that he seemed to be more cheerful, less worried. Once I asked him (waiting in vain for him to bring up the subject of his emotional state) how he was "doing." He answered "fine," a bit too abruptly, I thought. But we were having wonderfully spirited talks about spiritual matters, a direction that seemed to be a boon for both of us and I could always counter any professional anxiety I felt with what my parents used to say so often, quoting from Ecclesiastes, "To everything there is a season, and a time to every purpose under the heaven."

"A time" soon arrived: the sudden, sad breakup of the "old" civil rights movement, five years after it was born, with much attendant acrimony. My friend was especially hurt by all the suspiciousness and rancor which, out of nowhere, it seemed, spread into the discourse of men and women supposedly brothers and sisters in a common social and political effort. While my wife and I prepared to return North I heard my friend calling upon Simone Weil with a special urgency, and so did I soon enough—because she, more than anyone else we'd met in the course of our reading and studying, had in her own intense reflective way struggled with the greatest dedication to comprehend what makes people band together, then pull apart, and in so doing, begin to lose all respect for one another.

In *Gravity and Grace* one reads this: "Today we thirst for and are nauseated by totalitarianism, and nearly everyone loves one totalitarianism and hates another." And this: "The constant illusion of Revolution consists in believing that the victims of force, being innocent of the outrages that are committed, will use force justly if it is put into their hands. But except for souls which are fairly near saintliness, the victims are defiled by force, just as their tormentors are. The evil which is in the handle of the sword is transmitted to its point. So the victims thus put in power and intoxicated by the change do as much harm or more, and soon sink back again to where they were before." Volumes of such observations, sharp and almost frightening in their power, were her contribution to us—the many notebooks she kept, which only posthumously became books. She had a keen eye for idolatry, especially the secular versions many of us fail to regard as such: science or social science turned into religion, and a social activism which lacks the kind of moral and spiritual constraints she spent years trying to spell out in, among other writings, *The Need for Roots*. In her letter to Georges Bernanos she writes very much like the disillusioned English author of *Homage to Catalonia*: "One sets out as a volunteer, with the idea of sacrifice, and finds oneself in a war which resembles a war of mercenaries, only with much more cruelty and with less human respect for the enemy."

It would be deeply unfair to leap from the horrors of the Spanish Civil War to the moments of rancor and spite, the failures of charity, which took place in the midst of the civil rights struggle of the early 1960s—though, of course, a moment of smugness and arrogance, of callousness or discourtesy, had to be judged as such, no matter those "larger contexts" all too many of us conveniently call upon to justify our various sins of omission or commission. The point was that at a certain difficult time, when ideals once highly espoused had come crashing down—when white and black friends were shouting at one another as if segregation, the supposed enemy, had now become a triumphant reality—a young activist and his older friend had turned to Simone Weil, then dead about twenty years, for some help in understanding what had taken place.

Who was she, exactly, we now started to ask one another in admiration. Of course the adverb in the preceding statement reveals a serious error on our part; she is one of the most difficult intellectual figures of this difficult century to figure out "exactly"—and she would, without a doubt, have mocked the phrase "intellectual figures," she who wrote this: "A condition of any working-class culture is a mingling of what are called 'intellectuals'—an awful name, but at present they scarcely deserve a better one—with the workers." But she was indeed one, a person whose intellect worked feverishly and to enormous effect: her writing has helped many of us see more clearly what kind of world (culturally, politically, ethically, spiritually) we inhabit. Her contempt for the word "intellectual" (in this she is like George Orwell, who also tried to live among the poor and fight the fascists in Spain) had to do with an almost unnerving inclination she possessed for self-criticism, for the most unsparing analysis of her own situation in all its potential capacity for blindness, self-intoxication, presumptuousness: in brief, the sin of sins, pride.

Despite her constant assaults upon her own self, despite her doubts about the motives of many sorts of writers, she did take the risk of publishing some essays in the 1930s, and they revealed a thinker who had already spotted the monstrous Gulag in the making, long before Stalin's evil had been seen for what it was by many others on the "left." Was she, actually, on the "left," or the "right," or anywhere on one or another of our various political or ideological spectra? She reached out to the poor, wanted almost desperately to share their lot, tried working in several Paris factories and on several farms as a harvester, was earnestly antifascist (she was ready to die fighting the Falangists and later the Nazis), and hated with all her might the selfishly rich, the arrogantly powerful. And yet: her essays and letters and books also reveal her to be critical of Marx and Lenin and Trotsky and all sorts of socialist and communist verities or assumptions—both about what ails those of us who live in industrial societies and what might be done to make our lives better. That last word "better"—for her it meant something else than higher wages or membership in powerful, state-backed unions. She was, at the least, a moral philosopher, much interested in politics, yes; but really it was divine politics, so to speak, that was her passion. To call her "spiritual" is to acknowledge the intensity of her personal, passionate involvement in the life of Jesus Christ, and especially His last hours on earth—the Crucifixion, which for her was *the* edifying and redemptive moment in history. She was (I do not think I exaggerate) mesmerized during her final five years in a steady contemplation of God's visit among us. She wondered constantly what He experienced, what He learned about the creature called collectively "mankind," and through Him, what was both revealed and set in motion for all time.

Nor was Simone Weil inclined to shirk the social and political and intellectual implications of her religious nature as it revealed itself (was revealed) to her, hence her appeal to T.S. Eliot and many Christian theologians and philosophers. She was not afraid of words such as *la hiérarchie*, or *l'obéissance*, or *l'ordre*, or of the phrase *la propriété privée*. Early on, she was in certain respects an anarchist and pacifist; then she became a deeply spiritual political activist who dreamed long and hard about a post–World War II utopia (*The Need for Roots*) in which France's citizens would be both liberated from capitalism and immune from the temptations of fascism, state capitalism, secular liberalism, socialism, and communism, to name a few of this century's political and economic obsessions, if not nightmares.

Objects of idolatry might be the best phrase for all of the above, if one is to get close to the heart of her thought: she examined relentlessly twentieth-century idolatrous man—the unwitting spiritual hunger and the frustrated religious impulses that, finally, obtain expression in all sorts of political beliefs, social constructs, psychological theories, scientific postulates. Like Heidegger and Gabriel Marcel, and like such later novelists as Camus and Walker Percy, she was interested, always, in our struggle to find ourselves. We are the ones who, by dint of language and consciousness, are adrift in the universe: "Man is like a castaway, clinging to a star and tossed by the waves. He has not control over the movement imposed on him by the water. From the highest heaven God throws a rope. The man either grabs it or not." Those who have struggled with the abovementioned philosophers (and with Jaspers and Kierkegaard as well) will find the imagery familiar. And speaking of Kierkegaard, that exceedingly argumentative, troublesome, nettling, religious agent-provocateur, his *The Present Age* is echoed in Weil's notebook in this fashion: "Pride is the devil's characteristic attribute. And pride is a social thing." And a few entries later: "The Devil is the father of all prestige, and prestige is social. 'Opinion, queen of the world.' Therefore opinion is the devil. Prince of this world."

Her notebooks glitter with such Pascalian wisdom. As I started going through those notebooks about a decade ago I found myself, for the first time, keeping a series of notebooks myself: note after note written in response to note after note—the trouble being the succinct lucidity of many of hers, and the long-winded, exegetical pretentiousness of many of mine. There were, however, many notes of hers which I found utterly opaque, incomprehensible, and at times, I began to feel, murky, confused, even psychotic (that last categorization, perhaps, a measure of my own desperate ignorance, defensive pride, correct medical judgment, or possibly, a mix of all three). Here are some examples: "The docility of mathematical essences"; "Whence do we get commutativity?"; "What is purely a means is an ersatz form of the absolute end because of its ubiquity. Whence the comparison between the kingdom of heaven and a place. Money is an image"; "Suffering is nothing else but contemplating affliction with the mind."

Her entries attempt almost everything, it seems. She tries to analyze the nature of music and art. She delves into the Bhagavad Gita, shows her interest in folklore: African, Albanian, American Indian, Australian, Burgundian, Caucasian, Chilean, Chinese, Danish, Eskimo, Estonian, Finnish, Gypsy, Irish, Italian, Kobyle, Norwegian, Russian, Swedish, Welsh! She knows the Tibetan *Book of the Dead*, could read Tibetan, toward the end of her life tried (in London) to teach Tibetan to her friend Simone Dietz. Greek, Latin, and Sanskrit were obviously languages she could take for granted—and the abstruse language of higher mathematics, physics. Here is her mind at work during her brief stay in New York City, after the family escaped from occupied France, and before she left for London:

> Pan is the most ancient god; the first of the eight gods. Heracles is the first of the second series, of twelve gods. Osiris is the first of the third series. Then comes his son Horus. After that there is not another god.
>
> Heracles is 17,000 years before Amasis (whose date is about 569 B.C.). Osiris is 15,000 years before Amasis. So there were 12 gods from Pan to Osiris, or one god every $2000/12 = 1000/6 = 166\frac{2}{3}$ years. If the rhythm is constant, Pan precludes Heracles by $1000/12 \times 8 = 2000 \times \frac{2}{3} = 4000/3 = 1,333\frac{1}{3}$ years. The most ancient of the gods would be about 19,000 B.C. But there is no guarantee that the rhythm is constant.

During the early 1970s I tried to push aside entries such as the above in favor of the brilliant lucidity and (I thought, and still think) appropriateness and justness of her social and political writing. Hers was a *kind* of Christian socialism I find appealing, though I italicize the word "kind" because I know how fussy and unique she was as a thinker, and she has in that regard a right to be respected. She foresaw not only the brutalities of so-called communism (Russia, China), she also was prophetic in her analysis of the vicissitudes a statist socialism anywhere would face, even when its power is somewhat modified by a genuine electoral politics. Private property was for her a "need of the human soul," along with an equality of individuals before God and in each other's eyes—and so were "punishment" and "obedience" and "freedom of opinion" and "responsibility." She could be at once a militant radical and a fervent conservative; she could aim to sweep away exploitations of all kinds (commercial, social, racist, political) and yet insist upon "order," and, as mentioned earlier, "hierarchy"—as did Jesus, needless to say, when He distinguished "the last" and "the first."

For Simone Weil, in a society that obeyed Jesus, those vested with high authority would truly regard themselves as servants of those "ordinary people" whose work provides "goods and services"; and indeed the latter would feel themselves very much companions of the former (possessed of the same dignity and worth) in this rather limited voyage we take—as human beings on the planet Earth, that is. For her, one suspects, other voyages awaited, and for her also, I suspect, there was not enough time really to reflect upon how her dreams for hierarchy could come true, given the psychological and sociological and economic realities of this modern age. Who (using what power, and thereby at what cost to freedom) will begin taming our various competitive and acquisitive lusts, our consumerist preoccupations, our self-centeredness, our manipulative egoism? These aspects of so many of us Weil knew well, often analyzed (as in her marvelous essay "The Iliad, Poem of Force"), yet fails to heed sufficiently as she enunciates what (in fairness) is a dream she had for the victorious France of 1945, by which time she had been dead, at only thirty-four, for two years.

The immediately foregoing paragraphs (the quotes and the comments on them) remind me of the old days, of what had become for me, by 1972, a firm habit. We were living in New Mexico then, and I noted eagerly Simone Weil's acquaintance with Hopi myths, which I was myself getting to know. When I did work in Alaska among Eskimo communities I remembered her knowledge of Eskimo stories. Moreover, I was trying to figure out for myself what I believed, and had embarked (I realize in retrospect) on a series of biographical efforts, with the emphasis in each instance on the person's work, his or her writing rather than the details of the life, though I would, inevitably, give an account of some of those details. I wrote books about Erik H. Erikson, whose studies of Luther and Gandhi were so valuable and instructive; about William Carlos Williams and Walker Percy and Flannery O'Connor, three writers it was my privilege (or, in the case of O'Connor, my wife's) to know, and whose work I've found philosophically stimulating as well as of obvious high literary merit; and not least, about Dorothy Day and the Catholic Worker Movement, to whom and to which I have felt a close personal and religious connection. I had in mind one more such effort—to salute Simone Weil's astonishing contribution to our age's meditative possibilities. I'd written general essays about one or another aspect of her work, and several book reviews of biographical studies of her done by others. By 1978 I was well on my way, and even willing to talk with a publisher about the project. Yet it lingered and lingered, for me a first time, and I wonder why.

For one thing, I find myself at times terribly upset with something I read of Weil's—for example, her well-known denial of her Jewishness to the Vichy French authorities. I was about to quote some of her remarks on this vexing matter at length here, then discuss their implications, but, really, the point to register in this essay might go as follows: a brilliant mind, in my opinion, runs amok. I felt so when I first read the letter she composed on the subject, the gist of which is that the writer denies to these stooges of the Nazis that she is Jewish, and explains why. I use a number of Simone Weil's writings in two of my courses at Harvard, and invariably the students object—in fact, are incredulous—when they discuss that letter, as in this comment in a paper: "How can someone so intelligent write in that vein—given what she knew about the Nazis?" Another objection I hear from students, and sometimes myself: the "unreality" of her various agendas (as in *The Need For Roots*). She was a utopian, one quickly adds—but one morally haunted, if not moralistic. Hers was no mind bent on constructing "interesting" speculations about what *might* be. She desperately wanted to change the world in certain directions, and indeed, was prepared to die so doing.

Now, to a third matter, also posed often by students who have read biographies of Weil, and who often begin their questions with this introductory phrasing: "What do you, as a psychiatrist, think of her?" If I hesitate, or ask for clarification or amplification, we inevitably arrive at the last weeks of her life. Was she then anorectic, psychotic, a suicide? I pause, fret, qualify my remarks carefully, and depending on the day, the mood, the manner of the particular student's approach to the issue, answer in one of several ways. Usually I say what I've said in the essays I've written on Simone Weil—that she did indeed die young of tuberculosis, its clinical course decisively and for the worse complicated by her refusal to eat the amount of food needed to fight so serious an infection. That refusal was prompted, she maintained, by her wish to eat no more than the ordinary people of Nazi-occupied France were then eating. And some of those who have admired her and have written about her—Tomlin, for instance, whom I've mentioned earlier—make a point of that element of reality in the abstinence that, however, surely accelerated, if not brought about, Weil's death. What I've not had the heart (or stomach) to do in writing or with my students is get into a discussion of that particular patient's clinical demise as described by her doctors.

A separate essay would be required to deal with this vexing matter—her long-standing and complex avowal of indifference to food, her passionate way of maintaining that abstinence, and getting others (her mother, father, brother, friends, and alas and ultimately, doctors) involved in the question of what she intended to do, or rather, eat, and why. At the end of her life her doctors were exasperated, frustrated, and, one would imagine, rather angered. They declared her an anorectic suicide. Others have disagreed with such a medical designation, have pointed to her fierce determination, never lost, to fight the Nazis by returning to her homeland to join the French underground. The point is to emphasize, as I've already indicated (and have myself tried to do in various earlier essays) the actual circumstances of the time, the sacrifices many men and women were making, including what might be called the taking of "suicidal" risks. Still, such "suicidal behavior" was precisely that—connected to the relatively conventional activity of a military struggle. On the other hand, there *is* a tradition within Christianity (and other religions, too, especially Eastern ones) for ascetic contemplation and sacrifice—even self-sacrifice.

Here one is up against Weil's steadfast refusal formally to enter the Catholic Church, to which at the same time she felt strongly drawn. In this regard, her dying encounters with Father de Naurois (she'd asked to see a priest) are as edifying as her lamentable encounters at two hospitals with doctors and nurses. (She was for a while force-fed.) The good priest, who turns out to be, I think, perceptive enough to warrant being called inspired, described the patient as "a soul of rare nobility, a soul tormented to the depths by the mystery of God and the destiny of man, the mystery of Christ and Christianity." To that I would want to add "the mystery of her particular life"—its mixture of brilliant good sense and odd foolishness; its mixture of charm, vitality, moral energy, intellectual probity; and also the racking pain of migraine, the flights of fancy, the moments of unrelenting pride, one form of which, of course, was terrible self-abasement.

A year or so *before* she was hospitalized, she'd expressed herself this way: "Father, in the name of Christ, grant: That I may be like a total paralytic—wholly prevented from making any movement of the body, or even any attempted movement, that corresponds to any promoting of my will." No question the martyrs of the early Church who took themselves to the desert in prayer and repentance (in an effort she would describe as "decreation") were spiritual kin of hers—and yet one is stunned at this contemporary witness, and, I suppose, driven in horror to ask: why the need of it? Moreover, there is a terrific (and arguably perverse) willfulness at work in all this struggle for paralysis, even as the notion of "decreation" may be regarded as an ultimate assertion of self by means of the very effort to assault and demolish, once and for all, its hold.

In any event, I again allude to a subject that requires the chapter or two I haven't written, I'm indicating why: my troubled (I prefer that word to the now banal one, "mixed") feelings. And indeed, the priest who saw her at the very end says it as well as it can be said, says it out of his earned experience, not through the distance of time, and not with the remove of the cool intellect at work on, after all, a passionate trial of a particular human being. He referred to his "human annoyance"; he felt at moments that "the discussion she seemed to want was a waste of time"; he was, again, "annoyed" by what he called "a style highly abstract and abstruse, of a rapid dialectic, and very 'feminine,' under which I could feel deep instincts and tacit decisions perhaps hardly reflected upon, and which appeared to me to be travestied, dressed up in 'rationalizations' (as the modern psychologists say); in short, a thought that was elusive and at the same time prodigiously rich." At another point he also described her "thought" as "Judaic"—and yet, he remembers visiting her, giving her his sacerdotal blessing, "which she accepted with the fervor and humility of a great and experienced Christian."

So it went until the very end: the sturdy arguments that presented the one who formulated them with the danger of quibbling; and, at the same time, the crying desperation of a search, the intensely earnest "waiting for God"—a watch of sorts which at the same time could become a terrible ordeal for a given woman and others who loved her. I've found myself, upon occasion, utterly taken by her and her immensely arresting ego, both its intellectual and personal aspects. I've also found myself unable to figure out what I think of her—without, that is, amending or modifying what I've just concluded. At moments, I find myself becoming attracted to her—especially when looking at those lovely, fetching pictures of her, taken at the age of thirteen, where she appears full of sun, openhearted, even alluring. Soon enough, she would be wearing that huge cloak—often topped, though, by a beret worn at an interesting angle. Soon enough there would be no photographs of her, only one of her English grave.

I am also attracted to her restless energy—the European émigré in New York for only a few months, yet a visitor to Harlem's black churches (she loved the gospel music as she loved the Gregorian chants at the Solesmes monastery), and already set to visit Alabama and talk with sharecroppers. And I love her feisty independence, her capacity to walk alone, suspicious of "principalities and powers." She, too, belonged to the "homeless left," as Irving Howe has put it—in the company of such Europeans as Ignazio Silone and George Orwell. She, too, knew Dorothy Day's "long loneliness"— though, sadly, neither the (albeit passing) satisfactions of an extended life, nor those of having had a lover with whom a child was brought into the world, nor those of accepting the sanctuary of Mother Church. There is no peace, some of us believe, this side of Heaven—of which none of us can, needless to say, assume a future knowledge. All we can do is pray for forgiveness, even as we try to have the courage to keep going in our appointed tasks.

As I was finishing my book on Weil, I read a letter Dietrich Bonhoeffer wrote to his fiancée, Maria von Wedermeyer. Ironically, the letter was written on August 12, 1943, just a few days before Simone Weil died. Bonhoeffer, the German aristocrat and brilliant theologian, who dared fight the Nazis with all his might, was then confined to a concentration camp. Like Simone Weil, he had left the safety of America in 1939 to cross the Atlantic and take up personal arms against what he regarded as the worst of all evils. He was killed by the Nazis in April 1945, also still in his thirties. But dark as the world was in 1943 for Bonhoeffer, too, he wrote these words to his fiancée.

When I also think about the situation of the world, the complete darkness over our personal fate and my present imprisonment, then I believe that our union can only be a sign of God's grace and kindness, which calls us to faith. We would be blind if we did not see it. Jeremiah says at the moment of his people's great need "still one shall buy houses and acres in this land" as a sign of trust in the future. This is where faith belongs. May God give it to us daily. And I do not mean the faith which flees the world, but the one that endures the world and which loves and remains true to the world in spite of all the suffering which it contains for us. Our marriage shall be a yes to God's earth; it shall strengthen our courage to act and accomplish something on the earth.

Something in me kept reading and rereading that passage; I kept it on my desk as I looked at the various books of Simone Weil, and at pictures of her, and as I remembered her brother's remarks about her—her saintly vocation and her occasional moments of humor, as when she told him once that she'd kept a Jesuit up for hours in a most burdensome conversation. "God has put me here to do this to Jesuits, drive them to distraction!"

The contrast between Simone Weil at the end of her life and Bonhoeffer's affirmation of life at a comparable moment is all too striking. One wishes she had recognized the Old Testament beauty and wisdom expressed in Bonhoeffer's letter. One wishes that she might have forsaken some, just some, of that austerity, that headlong rush to a worldly exit, and stayed with us, nourished us with her splendid moral sensibility, and, finally, trusted God to know when her time had come. But such speculations about what might have been are a distraction from the work she accomplished, from the ideas and examples she left.

Dietrich Bonhoeffer

Who, knowing him as a child, a young man, even a young Lutheran pastor and theologian, would have predicted the course of Dietrich Bonhoeffer's life, its terrible foreshortening? He died (on April 9, 1945) in a German prison, killed as a convicted traitor to his country. He was only thirty-nine. And surely upon his birth (on February 4, 1906) or during his childhood and youth, such an outcome was beyond anyone's wildest imagining. Bonhoeffer came to be the person we now know and admire only in response to history's hard-to-predict unfolding. In a sense, after all, his moral testing, his spiritual fate, which so distinguished him from so many others, including thousands of Germany's Christian ministers, had everything to do with the triumph of Adolf Hitler and his Nazi thugs. Their political victory, in late January of 1933, was far from inevitable; it was, rather, a tragic result of betrayals, lies, deceptions, and deals that bewildered and staggered most of Germany's voters (a majority of whom had rejected the shrill, Austrian-born hate-monger).

How then do we understand the life of Dietrich Bonhoeffer, and especially the way in which it came to an end? Even as Hitler's rise to power was not inevitable, Bonhoeffer's arrest, imprisonment, and death were not the unavoidable conclusion to a religious (or ideological or psychological or social and cultural) drama. They could not have been foreseen by, say, 1933, with Hitler's ascent to power, or even in 1940, with his military victories evident and his authority at home a living nightmare for many—who, still, found ways of staying clear of the Gestapo, surviving the war, speaking with dignity and credibility to their fellow Germans, as Konrad Adenauer did. Indeed, in certain respects Bonhoeffer was an unlikely candidate for the role he eventually assumed, that of a principled fighter unto death against the German state. He was, after all, a Lutheran, for whom a nation's government deserves enormous respect, a matter of doctrine. Nor had Bonhoeffer grown up in a politically radical or culturally cosmopolitan home. His mother was from a renowned, accomplished family, whose members included a minister who belonged to the kaiser's court and a high military official, as well as lawyers and businessmen, titled members of the nobility. And similarly, his father was one of Germany's leading neuropsychiatrists, even as his relatives included jurists and individuals of the haute bourgeoisie. Dietrich was born in Breslau, but when he was six his father assumed an important position in Berlin, though, again, for all the intellectual ferment in the capital city, especially during the years of the Weimar Republic, the Bonhoeffers stood apart: a solid, stable, well-to-do family protected by its own largely secular values as well as its Lutheran loyalties from the moral and political skepticism that flourished in various Berlin circles and salons.

Dietrich Bonhoeffer was one of eight children. His oldest brother, Karl-Friedrich, would become a physicist. His older brother Walter was killed in the German army during the First World War. His brother Klaus, three years older, would become a lawyer—and would stand up to the Nazis, and be jailed and killed by them. His older sisters, Ursula and Christine, both married lawyers (Rüdiger Schleicher and Hans von Dohnanyi) who also passionately resisted Hitler's henchmen, and they too were arrested and killed just before the war ended. Bonhoeffer's twin sister, Sabine, married a lawyer and political scientist, Gerhard Leibholz, who was of Jewish ancestry, although a baptized Christian, and his youngest sister, Susanne, married Walter Press, a theologian. This was a family that lost four members to the Nazis, a moral resistance of a high order. The family also "lost" a daughter and son-in-law to exile in 1935, as the Nazis bore down relentlessly and viciously on anyone of Jewish background. Yet it was not a family whose interests and convictions, before the rise of Hitler, would seem to make it an all-out antagonist of his, ready to fight him (as the saying goes, and as it would happen) "unto death."

Hitler, actually, did not lack opponents who were of upper-class background, conservative in many respects, nationalistic, even (alas) anti-Semitic in their own quieter, more genteel fashion. The Nazis were by and large riffraff; and initially their appeal was to people who, despite their social and economic vulnerability, disdained and feared the left—the Weimar Republic's substantial socialist and communist presence. Hitler proclaimed *national* "socialism," a demagogic "populism" that offered the old consolations and satisfactions of hate: the Jew as the explanatory scapegoat. For certain upper-class Germans, connected to law and business and the military, Hitler's coarseness (and the crudities of his Nazi gauleiters) was obviously distasteful. A loose American analogy would be the contempt certain well-off, well-educated American Southerners had for the Klan, even as those same individuals had no interest at all in seeing blacks obtain even political (never mind social or economic) equality.

With Hitler's rise, needless to say, not only the Jews had to come to terms with what he stood for and, step by step, what he aimed to do and, very energetically, insisted on doing. Even many Jews thought power would tame Hitler, subdue his hysterical ranting, and curb the activity of his violence-prone followers. As for Germany's "Aryan" population, including its avowedly Christian members, Catholic and Protestant alike, it was soon enough effectively subdued by a totalitarian regime that brooked no opposition and got its way as it confronted anyone's doubts or misgivings with the full thrust of political power and with all that such control can do to exert its will. In fact, the quick accommodation of Germany's Protestant churches to Hitler tells volumes about the role of religion in the secular life of a twentieth-century industrial nation. Just as important was the role of the universities, for they too quickly made an amicable settlement with Hitler. In no time faculties were purged, books condemned and burned, and a host of leading intellectuals and their followers became public accomplices to or apologists for Nazi ideology. Or, more quietly, they fell in line with no inclination to express disagreement or qualms. Lawyers, journalists, physicians, teachers, ministers in droves became willing instruments of Hitler's various functionaries. Hundreds of ministers, on occasion, wore the Nazi brown shirt, embracing the Führer's leadership. In contrast, within days of Hitler's ascension as chancellor, Bonhoeffer spoke up, took on Nazism as idolatrous, spoke in defense of the Jews, and warned strenuously against the direction his nation was going—and in so doing, was cut off, actually, in the midst of a radio address.

How to account for such an early resistance, publicly expressed? In 1933 Dietrich Bonhoeffer was a twenty-seven-year-old pastor and theologian residing in Berlin and connected to university life as a teacher and a minister. He had become, already, a promising theologian: he had gone to Spain to minister to a German-speaking population in Barcelona, and he had spent a year at New York City's Union Theological Seminary. No question, he had already shown substantial evidence of a compassionate nature. In Barcelona, his heart went out to the working people, the unemployed in a nation even then contending with the conflicts that would bring to the fore Francisco Franco, one of Hitler's major allies. In America, Bonhoeffer would right away take note of *our* institutional racism (in 1930, before Hitler had come to power). He worried long and hard about a nation that segregated millions of its citizens, keeping them both apart and below: an affront, he saw clearly, to the readily espoused

Christianity of those who, nevertheless, had no apparent trouble with such a racial situation.

Yet, in other respects, he was obviously (at Union Theological Seminary, certainly) an almost quaintly conservative young visitor from abroad. Whereas the social gospel dominated the discourse at the seminary—the Great Depression was in full sway then—this young Lutheran of obviously genteel background was (at least intellectually) more interested in God than in man. Like Karl Barth, whom he admired, Bonhoeffer tried to comprehend what he acknowledged to be, finally, incomprehensible: God's reasons and ways. It is in our nature to do just that, to try to ascertain whatever we can of the Divine—and maybe all we can do is describe our yearning to do so, the futility of our search, and, perhaps, speculate on His will and even on His interests or wishes. The austerity (if not fancy) of such a posture must surely have struck some at Union Seminary (well into the twentieth century, after Darwin and Marx and Freud and Einstein, no less, not to mention the seeming worldwide collapse of capitalism) as remarkable, and not without social, cultural, and psychological implications: a flight to the unfathomable God of John Calvin as an alternative to an embrace of God's creatures, here at hand, in their all too obvious and profound suffering.

Not that Bonhoeffer himself was indifferent to the world of the here and now. He was an immensely likable, earnest man whose moral energy and evidently compassionate nature enabled him to get on well, indeed, with his American hosts. A devout Lutheran, he bowed to God's distant, unshakable power; a decent, approachable human being of good instincts and fine sensibility, he worried about his neighbors, of whatever kind, creed, or color. At Union, Bonhoeffer became especially close to Paul Lehmann, but to others as well; he carried them in his mind and soul. He corresponded with them throughout the dark days ahead, in the 1930s, and saw them all too briefly, at the end of that decade, just before the Second World War began.

Back in Germany Bonhoeffer would soon enough say good-bye

to the life of the young, promising theologian, the university-connected pastor and teacher and scholar, the Berliner of impeccable social background who played the piano brilliantly and who had also learned to play a very good game of tennis, whose family, amid the economic chaos of the 1920s, had never known the jeopardy, the doubts and anxieties, that descended on middle-class people, never mind the poor. Such people by the millions had turned to the communists or the Nazis, who were not only electoral opponents, but engaged in a fierce, unremitting battle for the streets of a proud, highly educated, industrial (and industrious) nation on the verge of political as well as economic collapse. On January 30, 1933, as a consequence of endless bargaining and manipulations behind closed doors, the very worst, the unthinkable happened. Hitler, on that day, became Germany's chancellor, and the fate of millions and millions of people the world over became sealed: for one reason or another they would be killed in the next twelve years, among them the then twenty-seven-year-old Bonhoeffer, who immediately made public his opposition to the Nazis.

Not that Bonhoeffer (or anyone else) knew how far in the direction of absolute evil the Nazis would take Germany and all of Europe. But he took a more accurate measure of those murderous thugs than others, and began to do so right away. He was, as mentioned, cut off speaking on the radio days after Hitler took office as he warned of the idolatry that would accompany the constant din of "Führer." Day by day, month by month, the Nazis engineered their totalitarian hold on the nation, and with it the flagrant racialism of anti-Semitism—a terrible echo, alas, that hearkened back over the centuries to, among others, Luther himself. But now those distant denunciations and, more recently, the Wagnerian descents into a self-importance that was purchased at the expense of others became something quite else: a state-sponsored hate with a killing aim. While his fellow ministers flocked to the Führer, Bonhoeffer and a relative handful of others became part of the "Confessing Church": on their knees they begged God's forgiveness for what was being said and done in their native land, even as they knew they themselves were risking their own situations, if not lives, by so doing. It was a time of great testing, a time when some fled, others submitted, still others began what would be the march of many millions to the concentration camps, the factories of murder that only an "advanced" technology in a nation such as Germany could enable and sustain.

Late in 1933 Bonhoeffer left Germany again, now for England. His opposition to the Nazis was clear and publicly known, but perhaps he needed time to figure out how he would enact it. Meanwhile, the Nazis accelerated their cultural (never mind political) control over Germany, so that when Bonhoeffer returned in 1935, the kind of work he did—the training of ministers in a tradition of prayerful opposition to the values being daily propounded by the Nazis and pounded into the minds of the German people under the adroit guidance of Joseph Goebbels—had become exceedingly dangerous. Nevertheless, in 1935, a Preachers' Seminary had opened, located first at Zingshof, on the Baltic Sea, and then at Finkenwalde, near Stettin. There, during the last years of Auden's "low, dishonest decade," wherein hell itself began summoning the German people, Bonhoeffer and a few others gathered, prayed, studied, and prepared themselves for what they must have surely sensed to be around the corner in their lives. Whereas the great majority of Lutheran pastors consented to Hitler's rule, even welcomed it and wore the swastika on occasion, Bonhoeffer and his associates said no to such an accommodation, if not an embrace. Instead they initiated a "Confessing Church," one at odds with established Christian officialdom. It was during these few years that Bonhoeffer wrote *The Cost of Discipleship* (1937) and *Life Together* (1939). In a way, he was divesting himself of the Lutheran legacy of a state-connected church and radically attaching himself to Jesus, who for him was now very much a living, constant ethical and spiritual guide. Even as Germany's clergy had become the Führer's self-abased "disciples," Bonhoeffer was exhorting his friends, his moral companions at

Finkenwalde, to stand fast with Jesus Christ, with all He upheld and passed on to others, His disciples. The "cost" would be a fearful isolation, a growing ostracism. But all in that community, all sharing that "life together," had already realized not only the intent of the Nazis, but their absolute determination to fulfill their own expectations at all costs. Hence the "cost" Bonhoeffer had in mind for himself and others like him: death if necessary, in pursuit of a committed Christian life.

By 1939 it had become clear that there was no stopping Hitler at home or, indeed, abroad, short of another world war. England and France had seen their desperate sell-out of Czechoslovakia at Munich come to naught. Now the Nazi beast was growling ferociously at Poland, and those two countries were feverishly preparing for the inevitable confrontation. At this point Bonhoeffer made his second visit to the United States. At Union Seminary he was a changed person: he had already been tested morally and personally the way few at that seminary, or any of us, get to be. He hadn't resisted Hitler in articles and signed petitions written in distant lands, in sermons delivered way out of the reach of the (even then) notorious Gestapo; rather, he had made crystal clear his principles within visiting distance of the Gestapo. Moreover, no sooner was he safely in America in June of 1939 than he was determined to return; he did so in July. Weeks later World War II would start, and his American friends would worry and wonder: why that hasty return, given the resistance he would offer and the consequent retaliatory response?

Why did he want so badly to go back to Germany? What did the "homesickness" of which he frequently spoke "really" mean? Was he not, perhaps, "depressed"? Might not he have been helped by some "conversations" with a "professional" person? Wouldn't it have been "wiser" for him to stay in America and help rouse a significantly isolationist nation to an awareness of what was at stake in Europe?

Once back in Germany he could not help seeing an implied meaning of the "homesickness" he suffered in New York City: his "home" was fatally "sick." With Germany at war all hindrances to

Nazi bestiality were lifted. The Nazi juggernaut across one national border after another was accompanied by a determination to pursue the wholesale murder of the Jews and of all others deemed "inferior" or "enemies" by a regime that was revealing itself, steadily, to be so monstrously evil as to have no parallel in all history. Bonhoeffer the resistor now plunged onward, the anti-Christ all around him. Through family connections he joined the Abwehr, the Military Intelligence, which for a while was secure from Gestapo surveillance. Thereby he did not have to fight in Hitler's legions, and thereby he in fact became a double agent, ostensibly working for Germany while he was plotting as best he could the defeat of Hitler. We are here in several senses on territory best described by Graham Greene or perhaps Joseph Conrad—the singular moral passion of someone who challenged conventional morality in its established political expression.

For Bonhoeffer, there was this huge religious irony: a Lutheran, he was now no longer in nominal opposition to the state; he was trying with all his might to lay it low   and in time, he would be arrested, imprisoned, and killed just days before Hitler's suicide. Even as Allied artillery and airplanes caused the ground where his prison stood to shake, he prayed, ministered unto others, and went to his death with a stoicism unforgettable to those who witnessed it. For him, surely, this was a "cost of discipleship" not discussed in writing, analyzed in arguments, worked into a polemical position, but assumed in the course of an intensely spiritual life. He was nearing his fortieth birthday and engaged to be married. The Nazis murdered him and others as a last gasp; within a month Germany (such as it then was) surrendered unconditionally to the Allied forces. One can only imagine what it was like, amid the ruins of Berlin, for Dr. and Mrs. Bonhoeffer and for Maria von Wedemeyer, their son Dietrich's fiancée (who had lost her father and two brothers to the war), to learn that he and his brother and his two brothers-in-law had been put to death during the last moments of the war.

The Devil came to Germany (through a devilish politics) in 1933, and this was not a Devil who came in slippery shoes, as the saying goes. Rather, this was a full-fledged, undisguised, head-on, modern, secular, statist version: mass murder become routine across the most "civilized" continent, in the cradle of historical Christianity—"the Rome-Berlin axis," as it was then known. Bonhoeffer's distinctive spirituality, that of a daily enactment of the moral truths spoken by Jesus and worked into His life, is our legacy (the terrible irony!) courtesy of that utterly devastating horror. Adolf Hitler gave us the Dietrich Bonhoeffer we admire and venerate today, a half century and more after his death at the hands of a Nazi executioner. "Prisoner Bonhoeffer, get ready and come with us," he was told by those who would soon thereafter kill him. And with that deed he "came" to all of "us." A long witness, a chosen ordeal at last ended—only to have a new existence, not only the heavenly one for which he aspired when he spoke the last words known to us ("This is the end—for me the beginning of life"), but the earthly one in which generations after him have shared. He was a man of faith now celebrated, his moral will such that it defied the dozens of evasions and rationalizations and self-justifications to which the rest of us are only too obviously and frequently heir. No question, to repeat, this man whose memory we continue to honor could have had it otherwise. He might still be with us, a revered and wise theologian and teacher, a onetime anti-Nazi activist, now in his early nineties, a person of intellectual achievement and moral stature.

George Eliot said farewell, unforgettably, at the end of *Middlemarch* (to the individuals whose complexity of mind and heart she had so subtly rendered) with these words: "Who can quit young lives after being long in company with them, and not desire to know what befell them in their after-years? For the fragment of a life, however typical, is not the sample of an even web: promises may not be kept, and an ardent onset may be followed by declension; latent powers may find their long-waited opportunity; a past error may urge a grand retrieval." Here is a shrewdly capacious psychology accounting for a secular dialectic in all its possibilities. Yet in Bonhoeffer we see little of the zig and zag so aptly evoked by a masterful observer of human psychology. In Bonhoeffer's life the march of his feet, step upon step, is directed, relentless, all too foretellable, an insistent and persistent and resounding antiphon of dissent to the legions of hate that paraded across Germany, then other countries: murder in constant motion (the whole world watching) inflicted by the militarily empowered dregs of our species. To such a fearsome anti-Christ, a would-be "disciple" of Jesus proved himself just that—and so, once more, the crucifixion story. By then Hitler was already in his bunker, on his way, one can only hope, to a future that even the greatest surveyor of our past and future, Dante, could never have imagined.

For many of us Dietrich Bonhoeffer belongs in the company of martyrs, men and women who have stood up, unto death, for their high moral and spiritual principles. Unlike others (we must keep remembering) who were forcibly rounded up and sent to death camps, he had every chance to avoid that fate. He might even have done so. He might have lived a secure, comfortable life and been highly regarded as one of the first Germans to see Hitler for what he was, to denounce him publicly, to lose his pastoral and professional positions—and only then, say, go into exile, as Barth and Tillich and thousands of other distinguished Germans did. Instead, he turned aside opportunity after opportunity to go abroad and to stay abroad in order to fulfill what he passionately believed to be his calling as a German, a Christian, one whose family had been treated so well over the generations by a nation that now in return required from its moral leaders, so he believed, everything they had to give. He did give everything, even as his Lord and Master had over nineteen hundred years earlier.

The psychology of the martyr is the psychology of will, of a decision made and its consequences be damned. In this age of determinisms, emotional and social and historical and economic, there is little room for will in the vocabulary we summon when we try to understand human affairs. Sometimes first things get overlooked in our rush for the less obvious. Erik Erikson, talking about

psychoanalysis and his study of Luther, once observed: "Willfulness often is regarded as a secondary trait—we rush to explain the
reasons for it. I believe some people have learned to be willful about
their beliefs—their willfulness is a big part of them, and it is summoned by them in pursuit of whatever it is they want to uphold.
Perhaps that is what 'leadership' is all about—the person who won't
take no for an answer: he believes something and he'll do everything
it takes to get across what it is he believes, and why. Others with the
same outlook—well, they aren't as committed to their ideals, or they
don't know how to stick to their guns, live up to their word, 'so help
me God,' as it's put."

To stand outside the gates of money and power and rank and approved success and applause, to be regarded as irregular or odd or
"sick" or, that final exile, as a traitor—such an outcome, in this era,
carries its own special burdens and demands: the disapproval, if not
derision, of colleagues, neighbors, the larger world of commentators
who meticulously fall in line with reigning authority, but perhaps
most devastating of all, the sense of oneself that is left in one's mind
at the end of a day. What *am* I trying to do—and is this, after all, not
only futile, but evidence that I have somehow gone astray? In that
regard, those of us who have been granted the right to decide what is
"normal" or "abnormal" ought be made nervous, indeed, by the likes
of a Bonhoeffer, as was the case, I suspect, even in 1939, when the
psychiatric manner of thinking held less sway than is now the case.

Arguably, all Christian theology is an effort to understand the
meaning of an individual quite provocatively eccentric, who was
put to His death, no less, as an utterly reprehensible criminal. As
if theologians haven't always had enough on their hands: to make
sense of someone whose words and deeds, speeches and proclaimed
ideas, stories and ways of being amounted (in the judgment of just
about everyone important and educated) to social and religious craziness. Now those same scholars have been required to take on an
individual who had the whole (conventional) world in his hands
and seemed driven to give it up in favor of an increasingly certain

confinement and extinction. "There was a lot of head scratching," Professor David Roberts kept saying to us at Union Theological Seminary, and therein lies an important aspect, indeed, of Dietrich Bonhoeffer's legacy. He became a modern martyr precisely because he dared to risk just such medical misgivings, just such ostracism, refusal, and condemnation, the highfalutin head-shaking at faculty clubs, the serious frowns at psychiatric seminars, perhaps even harder for him to endure than the actions of the Nazi police and judges, those flunkies of totalitarianism. Hence the way he strikes out in his later correspondence against his own (supposed) kind, the "psychotherapists" and "existential philosophers."

The heart of Bonhoeffer's spiritual legacy to us is not to be found in his words, his books, but in the way he spent his time on this earth, in his decision to live as if the Lord were a neighbor and friend, a constant source of courage and inspiration, a presence amid travail and joy alike, a reminder of love's obligations and affirmations and also of death's decisive meaning (how we die as a measure of how we have lived, of who we are). Bonhoeffer abandoned cleverness with language, brilliance at abstract formulation; he forsook denominational argument, oaths and pledges and avowals. In the end he reached out to all of us who crave, in hunger and in thirst, God's grace. And, one believes, unwittingly (how can it be otherwise?), unself-consciously, he became its witness, its recipient. His spiritual gift to us, especially, is his life. The principles he avowed and discussed in his writings gain their authority from the manner in which he conducted that life.

As two thousand years of Christianity come to an end, the witness of Dietrich Bonhoeffer, in all its near storybook drama, reminds us that if evil can be, as Hannah Arendt observed, "banal" in its everyday enactment, then good can be surprising in its occurrence, tenacious in its vitality, no matter the overwhelming odds against its survival. In the end, Hitler showed us a "heart of darkness," beating all too horribly fast, not in a distant jungle but right in our very midst, in our living rooms and our classrooms and, alas, even our churches and seminaries. It is just such a near-at-hand truth that Dietrich Bonhoeffer grasped right away, when others closed their eyes or calculated cravenly their immediate prospects. But he went that one further step; he remembered Jesus not intellectually or theologically or historically, but as our intimate teacher He meant Himself to be, the One who holds us to a certain moral and spiritual mark, and won't let go of us—if, that is, we are truly prepared, at whatever risk, to stay engaged with Him, to follow in His footsteps. This is the biggest "if" possible, and an "if" whose consequences, at the least, include the head-shaking of others, not to mention rejection, displacement, and worse. "I come to bring you not peace, but the sword," said this Visitor of visitors, signifying the severe disruption that a serious-minded faith, resolutely worked into a life, can prompt in someone who has signed up with such an Arrival, as it were: the Lord, no less, *here*, in our one and only mortal time of it, ready to take our hand and—no matter the turmoil, the hurt, and even the deathly pain—lead us to His *there*.

IV.

An Old One
and a Young One

Una Anciana

He is eighty-three years old. Once he was measured as exactly six feet tall, but that was a half a century ago. He is sure that he has lost at least an inch or two. Sometimes, when his wife has grown impatient with his slouch, and told him to straighten up, he does her suggestion one better and tilts himself backward. Now are you happy? he seems to be asking her, and she smiles indulgently. His wife is also eighty-three. She always defers to her husband. She will not speak until he has had his say. She insists that he be introduced first to strangers. As the two of them approach a door, she makes a quick motion toward it, holds it patiently, and sometimes, if he is distracted by a conversation and slow to move through, one of her hands reaches for his elbow, while the other points: Go now, is the unstated message, so that I can follow.

They were born within a mile and within two months of one another in Cordova, New Mexico, in the north central part of the state. They are old Americans not only by virtue of age but by ancestry. For many generations their ancestors have lived in territory that is now part of the United States. Before the Declaration of Independence was written there were people not so far away from Cordova named Garcia living as they do, off the land. They are not, however, model citizens of their country. They have never voted,

177

and no doubt the men who framed the Declaration of Independence would not be impressed by the boredom or indifference these New Mexicans demonstrate when the subject of politics comes up. They don't even make an effort to keep abreast of the news, though they do have a television set in their small adobe house. When Walter Cronkite or John Chancellor appears, neither of the Garcias listens very hard. For that matter, no programs really engage their undivided attention—and at first one is tempted to think them partially deaf. But the issue is taste, not the effects of age. Mrs. Garcia does like to watch some afternoon serials, but without the sound. She takes an interest in how the people dress and what the furniture in the homes looks like. The actors and actresses are company of sorts when Mr. Garcia is outside tending the crops or looking after the horses and cows. Nor is language the problem; they both prefer to speak Spanish, but they can make themselves understood quite well in English. They have had to, as Mrs. Garcia explains, with no effort to conceal her long-standing sense of resignation: "You bend with the wind. And Anglo people are a strong wind. They want their own way; they can be like a tornado, out to pass over everyone as they go somewhere. I don't mean to talk out of turn. There are Anglos who don't fit my words. But we are outsiders in a land that is ours. We are part of an Anglo country and that will not change. I had to teach the facts of life to my four sons, and in doing so I learned my own lesson well."

She stops and looks at the pictures of her sons that stand on top of the television set. Holding those pictures is an important function of the set, which was given her and her husband by their oldest son. Like his father he is named Domingo, but unlike his father he attended, though he did not finish, high school, in Española, on good days a ride of twenty or so minutes from the Garcias' home. Mrs. Garcia loves to talk about him: "I am a mother. You will forgive me if I am proud; sometimes I know I have been boastful, and I tell the confessor my sin. Domingo was a smart child. He walked quickly. He talked very well from the start. He did good work in school. We would take a walk, and he would point something out to me; often I had never noticed it before. Before he'd entered school he told me he wanted to become a priest. I asked him why. He said because he'd like to know all the secrets of God. It was my fault, of course. He would ask me questions (those endless why's all children ask—I later learned, after I had my second and third and fourth sons) and I would be puzzled, and not know what to answer. So, I would say the same thing my mother used to say to us: that is one of God's secrets. She died when she was ninety, and well before that my little Domingo had asked her when she would die. I lowered my head in shame, as I was taught to do when I was a girl, as I brought up my children to do, as thank God, my grandchildren now do. But my mother smiled and said, 'That is one of God's secrets.' After that, I think, I started to copy her words with my boy Domingo— though memory becomes moldy after a while and falls into pieces, like the cheese I make.

"I am taking you through side streets. I am sorry. Maybe we never know our own confusion; maybe it takes another to help us see what we have come to. I wanted to tell you about Domingo's teachers. They were Anglos. Today some of our own people teach in the schools, but not that many. Domingo was called brilliant by his teachers. They called me in. They said he was the only child in his class who was bright, and who belonged, really belonged in school. They made me listen to their trials with the other children they taught. I was young then, and obedient. I listened. Maybe now I would ask them please to excuse me, but I have to go home: the bread to make, you know, before supper. But my husband says no, even this very year we still would stay and nod our heads. Can you dare turn away from your child's teacher, just to satisfy your own anger? Our young people, our college students, say yes; but they live far away, under different conditions, not these here.

"The teachers never mentioned college to me. They weren't *that* hopeful about Domingo. I don't think they even thought about a person like us going to college. He just might be worthy of high

school, I was told. She had never before said that to one of our children, I was told. He is an exceptional boy, I was told. How did it
come about, I was asked. Well, of course, I smiled and said I didn't
know. She asked about Domingo's father: was he smarter than the
others? I said no, none of us are 'smart,' just trying to get by from day
to day, and it's a struggle. That was a bad time, 1930 and the years
right after it. Weeks would go by and we would see no money. (We
still see little.) And I had already lost four children: the last two
had been born in good health, but they died of pneumonia, one at
age two, one at age three. You can put yourself in my shoes, I hope.
Then, if you will just carry yourself back in time and imagine how
hard it was for us, and how little we knew, you will see that I had no
way of answering that teacher. On the way home I asked myself, *is*
young Domingo 'smart'? Is his father 'smart'? I was afraid to ask his
father that evening. He was so tired, so fearful we'd lose even the
land under us. He said he'd die and kill us, the child and me, before we went to a city and became lost. When I heard him speaking like that, I forgot the teacher and her question. I served him my
bread, and he felt better. Reassured, that is the word."

She stops and serves bread. She pours coffee. It is best black, she
says in a matter-of-fact way, but the visitor will not be judged for
his weak stomach or poor taste. She again apologizes for her fail-
ure to tell a brief, pointed, coherent story. Her mother was "sunny,"
was "very sunny" until the end, but she worries about "clouds" over
her own thinking. The two Domingos in her life scoff at the idea,
though. After the coffee she wants to go on. She likens herself to a
weathered old tree that stands just outside, within sight. It is autumn
and the tree is bare. She likens the coffee to a God-given miracle:
suddenly one feels as if spring has come, one is budding and ready
to go through another round of things. But she is definitely short of
breath, coffee or no coffee, and needs no one to point it out. "Tomorrow then."

In the morning she is far stronger and quicker to speak out than
later in the day. "Every day is like a lifetime," she says—immediately

disavowing ownership of the thought. Her husband has said that for years, and to be honest, she has upon occasion taken issue with him. Some days start out bad, and only in the afternoon does she feel in reasonably good spirits. But she does get up at five every morning, and most often she is at her best when the first light appears. By the time her visitor arrives, early in the morning by his standards, she has done enough to feel a little tired and somewhat nostalgic: "Each day for me is a gift. My mother taught us to take nothing for granted. We would complain, or beg, as children do before they fall asleep, and she would remind us that if we are *really* lucky we will have a gift presented to us in the morning: a whole new day to spend and try to do something with. I suppose we should ask for more than that, but it's too late for me to do so.

"I prefer to sit here on my chair with my eyes on the mountains. I prefer to think about how the animals are doing; many of them have put themselves to sleep until spring. God has given them senses, and they use them. Things are not so clear for us—so many pushes and pulls, so many voices; I know what Babel means. I go in town shopping and there is so much argument: everyone has an opinion on something. The only time people lower their heads these days is on Sunday morning, for an hour, and even then they are turning around and paying attention to others. What is she wearing? How is he doing with his business? Do we any longer care what the Lord wants us to know and do?

"I am sorry. I am like a sheep who disobeys and has to be given a prod. I don't lose my thoughts when they're crossing my mind; it's when they have to come out as words that I find trouble. We should be careful with our thoughts, as we are with the water. When I'm up and making breakfast I watch for changes in the light. Long before the sun appears it has forewarned us. Nearer and nearer it comes, but not so gradually that you don't notice. It's like one electric light going on after another. First there is dark. Then the dark lifts ever so little. Still, it might be a full moon and midnight. Then, like Domingo's knife with chickens, the night is cut up; it becomes a shadow of what it was, and Domingo will sometimes stop for a minute and say: 'Dolores, she is gone, but do not worry, she will be back.' He has memories like mine: his mother lived to be eighty-seven, and all her life she spoke like mine: 'Domingo, be glad,' she would tell him. Why should he be glad? His mother knew: 'God has chosen you for a trial here, so acquit yourself well every day, and never mind about yesterday or tomorrow.' We both forget her words, though. As the sun comes out of hiding and there is no longer any question that those clouds will go away, we thank dear God for his generosity, but we think back sometimes. We can't seem to help ourselves. We hold on and try to keep in mind the chores that await us, but we are tempted, and soon we will be slipping. There is a pole in our fire station. Once the men are on it, there is no stopping. Like them with a crash we land on those sad moments. We feel sorry for ourselves. We wish life had treated us more kindly. The firemen have a job to do, and I wonder what would happen to us if we didn't have ours to do. We might never come back to this year of 1972. We would be the captives of bad memories. But no worry; we are part of this world here; the sun gets stronger and burns our consciences; the animals make themselves known; on a rainy day the noise of the water coming down the side of the house calls to me—why am I not moving, too?"

She moves rather quickly, so quickly that she seems almost ashamed when someone takes notice, even if silently. Back in her seat she folds her arms, then unfolds them, putting her hands on her lap, her left hand over her right hand. Intermittently she breaks her position to reach for her coffee and her bread: "Domingo and I have been having this same breakfast for over fifty years. We are soon to be married fifty-five years, God willing. We were married a month after the Great War ended; it was a week before Christmas, 1918. The priest said he hoped our children would always have enough food and never fight in a war. I haven't had a great variety of food to give my family, but they have not minded. I used to serve the children eggs in the morning, but Domingo and I have stayed with

hot bread and coffee. My fingers would die if they didn't have the
dough to work over. I will never give up my oven for a new one. It has
been here forty years, and is an old friend. I would stop baking bread
if it gave out. My sons once offered to buy me an electric range, they
called it, and I broke down. It was a terrible thing to do. The boys
felt bad. My husband said I should be more considerate. I meant no
harm, though. I didn't deliberately say to myself: Dolores Garcia,
you have been hurt, so now go and cry. The tears came and I was
helpless before them. Later my husband said they all agreed I was
in the right; the stove has been so good to us, and there is nothing
wrong—the bread is as tasty as ever, I believe. It is a sickness, you
know: being always dissatisfied with what you have, and eager for a
change."

She stops here and looks lovingly around the room. She is
attached to every piece of furniture. Her husband made them: a
round table, eight chairs, with four more in their bedroom, the beds
there, the bureau there. She begins to tell how good Domingo is at
carving wood: "That is what I would like to say about Domingo: he
plants, builds, and harvests, he tries to keep us alive and comfortable
with his hands. We sit on what he has made, eat what he has grown,
sleep on what he has put together. We have never had a spring on
our bed, but I have to admit, we bought our mattress. Buying, that
is the sickness. I have gone to the city and watched people. They are
hungry, but nothing satisfies their hunger. They come to stores like
flies to sticky paper: they are caught. I often wonder who is better
off. The fly dies. The people have to pay to get out of the store, but
soon they are back again, the same look in their eyes. I don't ask
people to live on farms and make chairs and tables; but when I see
them buying things they don't need, or even want—except to make
a purchase, to get something—then I say there is a sickness.

"I talked to the priest about this. He said yes, he knows. But then
he shrugged his shoulders. I knew what he was thinking: the Devil
is everywhere, and not until Judgment Day will we be free of him.
I watch my son Domingo and his son Domingo; they both have

plans: next year we buy this, and the year after, that. Such plans are sad to hear. I try to tell them, but they do not listen. Those are the moments when I feel suddenly old, the only time I do. I turn to the priest. He says I am sinning: my pride makes me think I can disagree with the way the whole country works. I reply, 'No, father, just what I hear my own son and grandson saying.' Hasn't a mother got the right to tell her own flesh and blood that they are becoming slaves—that is it, slaves of habits and desires that have nothing to do with living a good life?"

She sighs and stops talking. She breaks her bread up into small pieces and eats them one by one. She stirs her coffee with a stick her husband made especially for that purpose: it is about six inches long, smoothed out and painted green. He jokes with her: one day she will decide to add milk to her coffee, because her stomach will demand it, and she will comply. Then she will really need the stick. But she has never used milk. Eventually she puts the stick down and resumes: "I am not a priest. I read the Bible, go to church, make my confession, and know I will soon need to come back to tell more. But a good life is a life that is obedient to God's rules, and a life that is your own, not someone else's. God and God alone owns us; it is not right that others own us. There are many kinds of slavery. My children would come home from school and tell me that they were glad they were not colored, because colored people once were slaves. 'Watch out,' I'd say. Their father would agree: you can become a slave without even knowing it. You can be white and have money, but not own your soul. I remember years ago I took the children to town; they were young and they wanted to see Santa Claus. He would come once and only once—and it turned out we missed him. Next year, I told the boys. They pouted. They beseeched me. They wanted me to take them somewhere, anywhere—so long as they could catch sight of Santa Claus. I held my ground. They would not stop. I said no is no. They said please. Finally I had to go after them. I talked as if I was giving a sermon in church. Maybe I ought not have spent so much of their time and mine, but I had to tell them,

once and for all, that we have our land, and we feed ourselves and
live the best lives we know how to, and we must never feel empty
and worthless because of a Santa, or because a salesman has beck-
oned us, and we have said No, I haven't the money.

"Later I wondered whether I'd done the right thing. I told my husband that Santa Claus is different. Children love him, and why not
try very hard to take them to see him? He thought for a while. When
he thinks he takes up his pipe and uses it more than he usually does.
With each puff I say to myself: there goes one of his thoughts—and
I wonder when he'll share them with me. Soon he does, though. It
never fails: he puts his pipe down, and then I know I'm to get ready,
and pay attention. I sit down and soon I hear. He always starts with:
'My wife, let me tell you what I think.' Soon I know what he thinks,
because he's not one to hide behind pretty phrases. As for Santa
Claus, Domingo told me what he thought of him: very little. I will
never forget his words. He said that Santa Claus has been captured
by the storekeepers. He said that they have him locked up, and he
will never be free until we stop turning Christmas into a carnival,
a time when people become drunk on their greed and take to stores
in order to indulge themselves. Of course, the priest lectures us in
the same way. And I know we all can be greedy. I eat too much of
my bread, more than I need. I shouldn't. Sometimes I punish myself: the oven is empty for a day or two—once for a week, after a
holiday. That time Domingo couldn't stand it any longer. 'I am
starving' he told me—even though I made him cereal and eggs instead. But bread for him is life, and I never stopped so long again.
I had made a mistake. A nun said to me, Punishment for a sin can *be*
a sin. If you are proud of yourself for doing penance, you are defeated
before you start."

She stops to open the window and summon her husband. Maybe
he should say exactly what he told his boys a long time ago about
Santa Claus. But no, it is hopeless; he will not come in until he has
finished his work. He is like a clock, so-and-so-many minutes to
do one thing, then another. The cows know the difference between

him and anyone else. He is quick. They get fast relief. When one
of her sons tries to help, or she, or a grandchild, it is no good. The
animals are restless, make a lot of noise, and Domingo pleads:
leave him his few jobs, then when he goes, sell the animals. As for
Santa Claus, forgotten for a moment, the gist of Domingo's speech
is given by his wife: "My children, a saint is in chains, locked up
somewhere, while all these stores have their impostors. Will you
contribute to a saint's suffering? Santa Claus was meant to bring
good news: the Lord's birthday is in the morning, so let us all celebrate by showing each other how much love we feel. Instead we
say, I want, I want, I want. We say, More, more, more. We say Get
this, then the next thing, and then the next. We lose our heads. We
lose our souls. And somewhere that saint must be in hiding, may be
in jail for all we know. If not, he is suffering. I tell you this not to
make you feel bad. It is no one's fault. We are all to blame. Only let
us stop. If we stop, others will not, I know. But that will be their sor-
row, not ours to share with them."

She is not ready to guarantee every word as his. He is a man of
few words, and she readily admits that she tends to carry on. Then,
as if to confess something that is not a sin, and so not meant for a
priest, yet bothers her, she goes further, admits to talking out loud
when no one is around. She is sure her husband doesn't do so, and
she envies him his quiet self-assurance, his somewhat impassive
temperament: "He is silent not because he has nothing to say. He
is silent because he understands the world, and because he knows
enough to say to himself: what will words and more words do to
make the world any better? I have wished for years that I could be
like him, but God makes each of us different. When our son Domingo went to school they began teaching him English. We had
learned English ourselves, enough to speak. But we didn't speak it,
only Spanish. When Domingo started learning English we decided
to speak it more and more at home. The same with the other boys.
Often I would rehearse my English by myself. I would learn words
and expressions from the priest and from the mayor of the town. He

was a cousin, and always doing business with Anglos. I learned to talk to myself in English—to my husband in Spanish, but to myself in English! Once my husband overheard me, and he thought I was delirious. He asked if I had a fever. I said no, none at all. He said I sounded as if I did. I said I was learning to speak English. He said he could speak English—but not to himself. Then he laughed and said, 'Dolores, you have spoken Spanish to yourself, too. I have heard you.' Since then I have been more careful, and I don't believe my husband knows that I still have the habit. I don't talk to teach myself English, though. I talk because my mind fills up with words, and then they spill out. Sometimes I talk with someone I imagine nearby. Sometimes I talk to myself. Sometimes it is in Spanish, sometimes in English."

After all the talk of talk, she has nothing more to say. She has to clean the house. She has to start a soup. She always has soup. As one pot begins to empty, she starts another going. It contains bones and vegetables. Soup, that is all it is called. Then she has to sew. There are clothes to mend, clothes to make. Her eyes aren't what they used to be, but with glasses she can see well enough. And finally, the radio. She prefers radio to television. She listens to music. She listens to the weather forecast and either nods or scoffs. Her sons hear the weather and actually believe what they hear. She knows better. She decides early in the morning what the weather will be like and only wants to know how good those weathermen are, with their gadgets and their reports from God knows what far-off cities. She feels sorry for them: they have a lot to learn. She hopes that one day they will go outside and look at the sky, rather than take their readings. It is one more bit of foolishness we have to live with now: "Years ago there were not these weather reports all the time. We would go out and size up the morning. We could tell. We felt the moisture before it turned to rain. If we had any questions we prayed, then more often than not we had an answer. I don't believe it was God's, either. The priest long ago warned us not to ask Him for favors, and not to expect His answers for the small favors we want. He is up there; we are down here. Once we are born, it is up to us. We pray to show our faith. If we have faith, we can do what is necessary. Not everything was good in the old days; we used to ask God's help all the time and be disappointed. My mother would pray that her bread came out good. I would pray for rain. I think we have stopped that, Domingo and me."

Now it is time to rest. Several times each day she and her husband do so. It is up to her to call him and she does it in such a way that he knows why. In a matter-of-fact way she speaks his name, and slowly he comes in. It is ten o'clock when they rest first. They lie down for five or ten minutes only, but that does miracles for them. They get up refreshed not only in body but in mind, and, evidently, soul: "I pray. I thank God for the time he has given me here, and ask Him to take me when He is ready, and I tell Him I will have no regrets. I think of all I have seen in this long life: the people, the changes. Even up here, in this small village, the world makes its presence felt. I remember when the skies had no planes in them, houses no wires sticking up, trying to catch television programs. I never wanted a refrigerator. I never needed one. But I have one. It is mostly empty. I have one weakness: ice cream. I make it, just as I make butter. I used to make small amounts and Domingo and I would finish what was there. Now I can make and store up butter or ice cream and give presents of them to my sons and their children. No wonder they bought us the refrigerator! As I lie on our bed and stare at the ceiling I think how wonderful it is: eighty-three, and still able to make ice cream. We need a long rest afterwards, but between the two of us we can do a good job. The man at the store has offered to sell any extra we have; he says he can get a good price. I laugh. I tell him he's going to turn me into a thief. It would be dishonest to sell food you make in your home for profit at a store. That's the way I feel. My husband gets angry: What do you mean 'dishonest?' he will say. I answer back: my idea of what is dishonest is not his. So we cannot go on about this. It is in my heart where the feeling is, not in my head. 'Oh, you are a woman!' he says, and he starts laughing. Later he will tell me that he was picking weeds, or taking care of our flowers, and he thought to himself: She is right, because to make food is part of our life as a family, and to start selling that is to say that we have nothing that is *ours*. It is what he always comes back to: better to have less money and feel we own ourselves, than more and feel at the mercy of so many strangers."

The two of them show a burst of energy after they get up. As they have rested, said their prayers, reminisced, they have given thought to what they will do next, and so, when they are ready, they set out decisively. It is almost as if they know they have limited time, know that soon they will again have to interrupt their working rhythm for lunch and another rest afterwards. "I am a new person several times a day," she points out, then adds right away, "But I can suddenly get quite tired." She feels "weakness" and "a loss of breath" come on, her way of describing the effects of a cardiovascular difficulty common to people in their eighties. Yet she sees no doctor, hasn't seen one in decades. "There are no doctors near here. I would have to go to Espanola. I would, if there was a need. I have pains all over; it is arthritis, I know. One can't expect joints to hold up forever. I do not believe in aspirin. I do not believe in medicines. I have to pant like our dog when I move too fast for too long. I have to stop and catch up. It is the lungs and the heart, I know. My son wants me to go get a checkup. My ankles swell at the end of the day, but the next morning they are down again. The body has its seasons. I am in the last one; winter is never without pain and breakdowns. I don't want to spend my last years waiting on myself and worrying about myself. I have already lived over twice as long as our Savior. How greedy ought one be for life? God has his purposes. I wake up and feel those aches and I notice how wrinkled my skin is, and I wonder what I'm still doing alive. I believe it is wrong, to ask a question like that. One lives. One dies. To ask questions with no good answers to them is to waste time that belongs to others. I am here to care for my husband, to care for this house, to be here when my sons and my grandchildren come. The young have to see what is ahead. They have to know that there is youth and middle age and old age. My grandson Domingo asked me a while ago what it is like to be one hundred. He is ten. I told him to be one hundred is to live ten of his lifetimes. He seemed puzzled, so I knew I had been thoughtless. I took him around. I put my hand besides his and we compared skins. I said it is good to be young and it is good to be old. He didn't need any more explanations. He said when you're young you have a lot of years before you, but when you're old you have your children and your grandchildren and you love them and you're proud of them. I took him around again and hugged him tightly, and in a second he was out there with his father and his grandfather looking at the cows."

She doesn't spend too much time with the cows, but the chickens are hers to feed and look after. She cleans up their fenced-in enclosure, and delights in their eggs. She and her husband have one hard-boiled egg each for lunch every day. She gives her sons eggs regularly; a nephew and niece also get some. She feeds the chickens leftovers, and some of her fresh bread as well. She is convinced that they lay better eggs because of her bread. One day for the sake of a visitor she borrowed a store-bought egg and compared it with one of hers: each was dropped in hot water for poaching, and hers did indeed stay much more intact and turn out tastier. "Animals today are turned into machines," she remarked after the experiment. She shook her head. She tried not to be gloomy, but she was worried: "No one my age has the right to demand that the world stand still. So much was wrong in the past that is better now. I didn't want this refrigerator, but it is good to have, now that I'm used to it. My grandchildren have had narrow misses with death, but doctors have saved them. I still mourn the babies I lost. Even if I'd been rich back then I might have lost them. Now there are medicines to kill the bad germs. But to see chickens or cows being kept in one place and stuffed with food that isn't really food—Domingo says they are fed chemicals—so they will grow fat all of a sudden, and have their eggs or become fit for slaughter: that is unnatural. I ask myself: Did God form the beasts of the field, and the fowl of the air so that they should be treated this way by man? I asked the priest once, and he scratched his head and said he would have to think about it. The next time I saw him I looked at him hard and he remembered my question. 'Mrs. Garcia, you don't make it easy for me,' he said. I smiled and said I didn't want to cause any trouble, but I can't help thinking about some of these things. He answered. 'I don't know what to say.' Then I decided I'd best not trouble him any more. He once told me that a priest only knows what Christ promised us; how He will bring about His promises—that's not for man to know. I thought afterwards I ought to confess to him my boldness—the sin of pride. Who am I to decide they have no right to run those chicken farms? But God forgive me, I still believe it is wrong: I still believe animals ought not to be turned into machines."

She arranges the eggs she brings in very carefully; she takes them out of her basket and puts them in a bowl. Some are brown, some white. She likes to fix them up like flowers; they give a freckled appearance from afar. When she uses some, she rearranges those that are left. She handles them not only with care but with pride and affection. Sometimes as she talks and does her work with the eggs she will hold a warm one in her hand: "I feel comforted by a fresh egg. It is sad to feel it get colder, but that is life. My grandaughter loves to help me collect eggs. The other day she asked me if the eggs inside a woman are the same kind as those that come out of a chicken. I was taken aback. I told her I didn't think so. Then I wondered what else to say. My husband said later there isn't anything more to say. The priest agreed. I felt I'd failed the little girl, though: I changed subjects on her before she even knew what had happened. A few minutes later I could tell her mind was back with the eggs, and she wanted to ask me more questions. But I wouldn't let her. I didn't tell her no, at least not directly. I just kept up my line of chatter. The poor girl, she was overcome by her grandmother's words—and by her own shyness! This time I didn't go to the priest later and ask him what I should have said. I have never talked to him about such matters. When one is young they are too personal; and besides, what is there to ask, and what is there to say? Also, a priest is entitled to respect: they are not living a worldly life, and there is much they don't know. I think our new priest is like a youth, even if he is fifty; I mean, he has never tasted of life. That is what a priest is about, of course; his passions go up toward the altar, and then to Heaven. So, I sat and thought about how to talk with my granddaughter the next time. I hope I can do her some justice. Time will tell. One never knows what to say except when the moment is at hand. I do rehearse conversations sometimes, though, I have to admit."

She stops abruptly, as if this is one conversation she doesn't want to pursue. Anyway, she has been dusting and sweeping the floor as she talks and now she is finished. Next come the plants, a dozen or so of them; they need to be watered and moved in or out of the sun. She hovers over them for a minute, doing nothing, simply looking. She dusts them, too. She prunes one: "I've been waiting for a week or so to do this. I thought to myself: that plant won't like it, losing so much. I dread cutting my toenails and fingernails. I am shaky with scissors. But I go after the plants with a surer touch. They are so helpless, yet they are so good to look at. They seem to live forever. Parts die, but new parts grow. I have had them so long—I don't remember the number of years. I know each one's needs, and I try to take care of them the same time each day. Maybe it is unnecessary nonsense, the amount of attention I give. I know that is what Domingo would say. Only once did he put his belief into words, and then I reminded him that he has his habits, too. No one can keep him from starting in one corner of his garden and working his way to the other, and with such care. I asked him years ago why not change around every once in a while and begin on the furthest side, and go faster. 'I couldn't do it,' he said, and I told him I understood. Habits are not crutches; habits are roads we have paved for ourselves. When we are old, and if we have done a good job, the roads last and make the remaining time useful: we get where we want to go, and without the delays we used to have when we were young. How many plants died on me when I was first learning! How often I forgot to water them, or watered them too much because I wanted to do right. Or I would expose them to the sun and forget that, like us, they need the shade, too. I was treating them as if they needed a dose of this, a trial of that. But they have been removed from God's forests, from Nature it is; and they need consideration. When we were young my husband also used to forget chores; he'd be busy doing one thing, and he'd overlook the other. But slowly we built up our habits, and now I guess we are protected from another kind of forgetfulness: the head tires easily when you are our age, and without the habits of the years you can find yourself at a loss to answer the question: what next?"

She turns to lunch. She stirs the soup. She warms up the bread. She reaches for the eggs. She sets a simple, careful table, a large spoon and a knife for herself, her husband, and their guest. Each gets a napkin from a set given her half a century ago by her mother, and used on Sundays, holidays, special occasions. She is apologetic: "I fear we often look at these napkins but don't use them. No wonder they survive so well! They remind us to behave ourselves, because it is no ordinary day; and so, we eat more carefully, and don't have to use them. They are usually in the same condition when I put them away as when I took them out. My grandmother made them, gave them to my mother, and now I have them. My three daughters died as infants; I will give the napkins to my eldest son's wife. I tried to do so when they were married, but she said no. I insisted, and only got more refusals. If she had been my daughter, she would have accepted. But I was not hurt. It takes time to move over from one family and be part of another. She would accept the napkins now, but they would become frightened if suddenly I offered them. Is she sick? Does she know something we don't know? What have we done to neglect her, that she offers us what she loves to put on her own table? So, I will have them until the end, when all possessions obtain new masters."

She has to go outside. It is cold and windy, but sunny. There is some fresh milk there in a pail—from cows which, she hastens to add, present no danger of sickness to a visitor who up until that moment had taken for granted the word *pasteurized* that appears on every milk bottle or carton. And she has herself and her husband as proof—a touch of reassurance which she obviously enjoys being able to offer: "My sons' wives sometimes hesitate, too. I can see what they think on their faces. They deny it, but I know: Is it safe to drink milk right from the cow? They are from the city, and they have no way of understanding that many cows are quite healthy; their owners know when they are sick. Anyway, Domingo and I survived without store milk, and we are not young, and not so sick we can't work or eat—or drink milk."

She wraps herself in a sweater she has made and upon opening the door quickly turns back for a moment: "Oh, the wind." But she persists, and is gone. When she is back, she resumes where she has left off: "The wind can be a friend or an enemy. A severe wind reminds us of our failures: something we forgot to fasten down. A gentle wind is company. I have to admit, I can spend a long time listening to the wind go through trees, watching it sweep across the grass. Domingo will come in and say, 'Oh, Dolores, come out and watch the wind go through the grass.' I hurry out. I often wonder if the ground feels it—like hair being combed and brushed. I walk with our dog and he gets scents from far off, carried by the wind. I tell him not to be tricked. Better to let things quiet down, then take another scent. He is over ten, and should not run long distances. He doesn't know his own limits. But who does, exactly? It takes a lifetime to get used to your body, and by the time you do, then it is almost time to say good-bye and go elsewhere. I often wonder whether the wind carries our soul skyward. It is another of my foolish ideas, and I put it to the priest long ago—not this one, but the one who came before him. He was annoyed with me. 'Mrs. Garcia,' he said, 'you have an active imagination.' I apologized. He reminded me that God's ways are not ours. I wanted to tell him that the wind comes mysteriously from above and might be one of many good, strong arms our Lord has. But I knew to keep quiet was best. He was a very stern priest, and outspoken. He would not have hesitated to dress me down severely and warn me publicly that I would pay for that kind of talk in Hell. Once he cuffed my husband because Domingo told him he'd heard that much of our weekly collection was going to Africa or Asia, to places way off, and meanwhile so many people hereabouts are without work and go hungry.

"It was in the bad years, in the 1930s. We were poor, but at least we had our land. Others had nothing. And the priest was fat. He was waited on, and he dined on the best; we were told that by the woman who cooked for him. Mind you, she did not serve him. He had to have someone special to do that. And he paid them a pittance. They had children they were supporting; and, alas, husbands too. In a good mood he would promise them an eternity in Heaven. On bad days he would threaten them with Purgatory and no escape—so, of course, they would leave his kitchen in tears, clutching their rosary beads all the way home. My husband heard of this, and was enraged. He said terrible things. I pleaded with him to stop. We were so poor, and the bank threatened to take away our small farm. Some people had thought of marching on the bank. The bank officials heard of the plan and never made a move against us. By then I had lost four children. I will not repeat what Domingo said about the priest—or the Church. The worse his language, the harder I prayed. I kneeled by my bed and prayed one evening after he had carried on a full hour, it seemed; it must have really been a few minutes, I now know, but I thought he would never stop. Then a heavy wind came, later that evening, and I was sure: God was approaching us to exact his punishment. And why not, after Domingo's outburst? He was tidying up outside. He had calmed down. I had heard him say a Hail Mary, but I pretended to be lost in my own work. He didn't want me to know that he had taken back the words he had spoken; he is proud. I decided to pray for him, but I was sure something bad would happen. Nothing did, though; the wind came, then left. A week afterwards I told Domingo of my fears. He laughed and said we are too intelligent, both of us, even without education, to be superstitious. I agreed. But a month later he came in one day for lunch and he told me he had to confess something to me. I said, Not to me, to the priest. No, he had very little to tell that priest, only the briefest of admissions once a month. I said nothing. He said that he'd been afraid too, that evening after he'd lost his temper. When the wind came, and he was outside, and the horses started whinnying and the dog ran back and forth, he did not know what to do or why the animals were upset; so he had gotten down on his knees and asked God's forgiveness. He'd even asked Him to take us both, with the house: through a tornado, perhaps. But soon it became very still, and I think each of us must have been holding our breaths, without knowing we were doing so together, like so much else we do! I fear that when he goes, I will, or when I go, he will. But I have no right to such thoughts: it is not up to me or to Domingo, but to our Lord and Savior. We are sinners, though, and we can't help being selfish. There will be no future for either of us alone. I only hope we are not tested by being separated for too long by death!"

When her husband comes in, without being called, she says that it is now noon. They go by the sun. They have a clock in their bedroom, but they rarely use it. They forget to wind it, except when their son is coming and they want to show him that they like his present: "Domingo gave us the clock, and I treasure it. I look at it and think of him. We only have two sons. It is nice to be reminded of them. I don't mean to sound as if I pity myself. Our son Domingo works at Los Alamos. He says it is maintenance he does; he looks after all those scientists. They leave their laboratories in a mess, and someone has to pick up after them, or everything would stop cold one day. He gets a good wage, and jobs are few around here, so he is lucky to be there. He could have stayed with us, worked on the land. But all we have is our animals and the crops—no money. I put up many jars for the winter, but jars of food are not enough to attract young people, and I see their view. There are a hundred like Domingo who would like his job. Before they brought in the laboratories at Los Alamos, there was nothing anywhere near here.

Domingo would be in Albuquerque, I believe, if it hadn't been for Los Alamos. My younger son is down there. I've never even been to Santa Fe. He drives up here on weekends. His life is difficult, living in the city. I don't ask him much; I wouldn't understand. His wife longs to come back here. He does, too. But how can they? No work. Domingo was interviewed several times for his job. He took a test, I believe. He did well. The teachers who predicted good for him, they were right. It's too bad he didn't finish high school; the war came, the one against Japan and Hitler.

"Then came the next war. My second son, Francisco, went to Korea. He was there for many months. I remember well the Saturday morning that I got news of him. I remember the day he came home. I was sitting in this very chair. I had to mend some of my husband's clothes. I was almost through, and as it does, my mind was already preparing for the next step in the day: a visit outside to pick some tomatoes. Suddenly the door opened, with no warning. Who could it be—the front door, hardly ever used, rather than the side one right here? My boy Domingo—he lived with us then, and worked as a handyman in the school where they had always thought so well of him. He had his suit on. 'Domingo,' I said, 'why the suit?' He did not answer. For a second I wondered how he had slipped in and put it on without my knowing. We will do anything not to see what is right before us. I believe I might have wondered and wondered about such petty questions—but after Domingo came his father, also with a suit on. I got up and shouted, 'It is not Sunday!' I said it over and over again. 'It is not, it is not!' Then I started crying. They never told me. I never asked. I just knew. My husband asked me if I wanted to change my dress. I said no. I am a plain woman, and my son was a plain man—no pretenses. He did not die in his Sunday clothes. They turned around and I followed them. We walked down that road, two miles. I saw nothing. I heard nothing. I was alone, even though they were with me, one on each side. Once I must have looked near collapse. I felt their hands and was surprised to see them standing there. Then I dropped my beads. I picked them up, but

I didn't say the Rosary. I just kept holding onto the beads. They had brought the body to the basement of the school building, a United States flag around it. Later, after the funeral, they wanted to give me that flag; I said no, it could stay at the school. Let the children see what war means. That is something they should learn—as much as how to read and write and count. It is no good when flags are used that way."

She has gone too far to suit her sense of propriety. She insists upon her ignorance. Who is she to talk about wars? They come about through events she has no knowledge of. She has a place in God's scheme of things; best to stay in it. But something makes her restless, no matter how she tries to put aside her doubts and misgivings. She stands up, walks toward her plants, and examines them, one by one. They are all right. She goes back to her chair. Then she is up offering coffee, serving a delicious chocolate marble cake she has made—from a packaged mix, a concession on her part to her daughter-in-law's urging. Once again seated, she interrupts a conversation about the "new road"—the road in front of her house which now for the first time is paved—to put into words what she can't stop thinking about: "There was another time. Two years ago, before that road was fixed up to be so strong it can ignore the weather, I had walked down to talk with my neighbor. She had suffered badly from pneumonia, but was on the mend. As I came toward the house I saw them again. You know, this time I thought my mind had left me. I wiped my eyes, but they wouldn't go away. I called to them, but they didn't answer, so I was sure they weren't there. It was late afternoon, a time when shadows begin to appear, and one can be fooled, anyway. So I wiped my eyes again, and when they remained, I looked around, hoping to see them in back of me, too. Then I would know; my eyes, my head—something for a doctor to heal, or a warning from God that it won't be long. Well, soon they were upon me; it was only when I *felt* them that I believed they were there and I was there. I remember thinking that perhaps I'd fallen asleep at my neighbor's, or maybe I'd taken a nap at my own house and now was waking up. In a second one can have such thoughts. In another second one can know everything without hearing a word. I said, 'How did it happen?' My husband couldn't talk. I held on to him and wanted him to tell me, but he was speechless. My son tried to tell me, but he couldn't finish his story. He used the word 'car,' and that was enough for me. Later they tried to give me the details, and I begged them to stop. Those suits on a day in the middle of the week! There have been days since when I have wanted to burn those suits or tear them to shreds. There have been days when I have lost all faith. I dared not go to confession, I could not let a priest hear what was on my mind. I cringed before God, knowing He hears everything, even what is not spoken but crosses the mind, a rabbit of an idea, suddenly upon you, quickly chased away, but back again in an unsuspecting moment, when all is quiet."

With that she stopped talking and looks out the window. What ought a visitor do—sit still and wait or find an excuse to leave immediately? Suddenly, though, she is talking again, a bit more softly and slowly and reflectively, but with no apparent distress. And she seems to want to talk: "The mountains, our mountains—I look at them when I need an anchor. They are here. They never leave us. Birds come, stay a while, leave. The moon is here, then gone. Even the sun hides from us for days on end. Leaves don't last, nor flowers. We have had a number of dogs, and I remember them in my prayers. But those mountains are *here*. They are nearer God than us; sometimes I imagine Him up there, on top of one or another mountain, standing over us, getting an idea how we're doing. It is wrong to think like that, I know. But a poor old woman like me can be allowed her foolishness. Who is without a foolish hope? Who doesn't make up dreams to fit his wishes? Sometimes I walk up toward the mountains. I can't go as far now as before. I don't tell my husband I'm going; he would worry that I'd lose my breath completely and no one would be around. But I pace myself, and, as I say, I have to be content with approaching those hills.

"The other day I walked toward them and there was a meeting on the side of the road. I stopped and listened. I never went any further. They were our young men, and some people from the city. *Chicanos,* they spoke of Chicanos. We are Chicanos; nothing else will do, they said. I came home and told my husband. Yes, he said, we are Chicanos. We are so many things, he said. 'Mexican American,' 'Mexicano,' they'd call my boys at school, those Anglo teachers. I would say nothing. They thought then it was their right to call us what they pleased. Spanish, we are Spanish. Many of us may have some Indian blood, too. But I will tell you: I am a woman and a mother and Domingo a man and a father, and both of us belong to this country and no other, and we owe allegiance to the state of New Mexico. Should we give ourselves one name or another, or should we get each day's job done? I can't believe Christ wants us to be Anglo against Chicano, or Chicano against Anglo; but the world is full of bitterness, and when will there be an end to it, *when?* I wondered while I walked home. It is a bad thing to say, but I was glad to come upon that meeting; it took my mind off myself and my memories. I saw that others want to know why there is so much injustice in the world. For a few days after my son was killed in the accident I wondered again whether God cared. I know He is there, watching over us; but I would wake up in the night and my forehead would be wet and I would be shaking. I had dreamed that God had fallen asleep, and so we all were going to suffer: the Devil would win his fight. I thought of those days, now gone, while I listened to the young people shouting 'Chicano!' They mentioned all the bad, nothing good; Domingo says that is how it goes when people have been hurt, and I nodded, because I remembered how I once felt."

One morning, in the midst of a conversation, she scolds herself for talking too much. She falls silent. She glances up at the picture of Christ at the Last Supper. Her face loses its tension. She slumps a bit, but not under the weight of pain or even age. She feels relaxed. There are a few dishes to wash. There is a curtain that needs mending. There is not only bread to make, but pies. Her grandchildren love her pies, and she loves seeing them eaten. "Children eat so fast," she says with a sigh of envy. She begins talking again. She resumes her activity. She has to pick at her food now. "When one is over eighty the body needs less," she observes—but immediately afterwards she looks a little shy, a little apprehensive: "I have no business talking like a doctor. Once the priest told me I talk like him. I told him: I have raised children; it is necessary at times to give them sermons, and hear their confessions. He smiled. If I had another life I would learn to be a nurse. In my day, few of our people could aim so high—not a woman like me, anyway. It is different today. My sons say their children will finish high school and my Domingo in Los Alamos says *his* Domingo does so well in school he may go on to a college. I laugh with my husband; a Domingo Garcia in a college. Maybe the boy will be a doctor. Who knows? He likes to take care of his dog. He has a gentle side to him. He is popular with the girls, so I don't think he's headed for the priesthood. He tells me he'd like to be a scientist, like the men his father looks after in the laboratories. I worry that he would make those bombs, though. I wouldn't want that on his conscience. My son told me they do other things there in the laboratories, not just make bombs. I said, 'Thank God!'

"Of course all of that is for the future. I don't know if I will be around to see my grandchildren have children of their own. One cannot take anything for granted. The priest laughed at Domingo and me last Sunday, and said, 'You two will outlast me; you will be coming here when you are both over one hundred.' I said, 'Thank you father, but that is a long way off, to be a hundred, and much can happen.' 'Have faith,' he said, and he is right: one must."

She pauses for a few seconds, as if to think about her own admonition. Then she is back on her train of thought: "Sometimes after church Domingo and I walk through the cemetery. It is a lovely place, small and familiar. We pay our respects to our parents, to our aunts and uncles, to our children. A family is a river; some of it has passed on and more is to come, and nothing is still, because we all move along, day by day, toward our destination. We both feel joy in our hearts when we kneel on the grass before the stones and say a prayer. At the edge of the cemetery near the gate is a statue of the Virgin Mary, larger than all the other stones. She is kneeling and on her shoulder is the Cross. She is carrying it—the burden of her Son's death. She is sad, but she has not given up. We know that she has never lost faith. It is a lesson to keep in mind. We always leave a little heavy at the sight of our Lord's mother under such a heavy obligation. But my husband never fails to hold my arm, and each Sunday his words are the same: 'Dolores, the Virgin will be an example to us this week.' It is as if each Sunday he is taking his vows—and me, too, because I say back to him, 'Yes, Domingo, she will be an example to us.' Now, mind you, an hour later one of us, or both of us, will have stumbled. I become cranky. Domingo has a temper. I hush him, and he explodes. He is inconsiderate, and I sulk. That is the way with two people who have lived together so long: the good and the bad are always there, and they have become part of one life, lived together."

She hears his footsteps coming and quickens her activity a bit. She will not be rushed, but he needs his coffee and so does she. Often she doesn't so much need it as need to drink it because he is drinking it. He lifts his cup, she follows; he puts his down, and soon enough hers is also on the table. Always they get through at the same time. This particular morning Domingo is more expansive and concerned than usual—a foal has just been born. "Well, enough. I must go check on the mother and her infant." He is up and near the door when he turns around to say good-bye: "These days one never knows when the end will come. I know our time is soon up. But when I look at that mother horse and her child in the barn, or at my children and their children, I feel lucky to have been permitted for a while to be part of all this life here on earth." His hand is on the door, and he seems a little embarrassed to have spoken so. But he has to go on: "I am talking like my wife now! After all these years she sometimes falls into my silences and I carry on as she does. She is not just an old woman, you know. She wears old age like a bunch of fresh-cut flowers. She is old, advanced in years, *vieja*, but in Spanish we have another word for her, a word which tells you that she has grown with all those years. I think that is something one ought hope for and pray for and work for all during life: to grow, to become not only older but a bigger person. She is old, all right, *vieja*, but I will dare say this in front of her: she is *una anciana*; with that I declare my respect and have to hurry back to the barn."

Ruby Bridges

A well-developed conscience does not translate, necessarily, into a morally courageous life. Nor do well-developed powers of philosophical thinking and moral analysis necessarily translate into an everyday willingness to face down the various evils of this world. I was once helped in the effort at clarification by a black woman whom I suppose I'd have to call illiterate. She pointed out that "there's a lot of people who talk about doing good, and a lot of people who argue about what's good and what's not good." Then she added that "there are a lot of people who always worry about whether they're doing right or doing wrong." Finally, there are some other folks: "They just put their lives on the line for what's right, and they may not be the ones who talk a lot or argue a lot or worry a lot; they just *do* a lot!"

Her daughter happened to be Ruby Bridges, one of the black children, who, at age six, initiated school desegregation in New Orleans against terrible, fearful odds. For days that turned into weeks and weeks that turned into months, this child had to brave murderously heckling mobs, there in the morning and there in the evening, hurling threats and slurs and hysterical denunciations and accusations. Federal marshals took her to school and brought her home. She attended school all by herself for a good part of a school year, ow-

ing to a total boycott by white families. Her parents, of sharecropper background, had just recently arrived in the great, cosmopolitan
port city—yet another poor black family of rural background trying
to find a slightly better deal in an urban setting.

Still, Ruby persisted, and so did her parents. Ruby's teachers
began to wonder *how come*—about the continuing ability of such
a child to bear such adversity, and with few apparent assets in her
family background. I reassured those teachers, I regret to say, with
the notion that all was not as it seemed. Ruby appeared strong, but
she would, soon enough, show signs of psychological wear and tear.
Perhaps she was "denying" her fears and anxieties; perhaps her
strange calm in the face of such obvious danger represented a "reaction formation." Then there was this bit of information: "I was
standing in the classroom, looking out the window, and I saw Ruby
coming down the street, with the federal marshals on both sides
of her. The crowd was there, shouting, as usual. A woman spat at
Ruby but missed; Ruby smiled at her. A man shook his fist at her;
Ruby smiled at him. Then she walked up the stairs, and she stopped
and turned and smiled one more time! You know what she told one
of the marshals? She told him she prays for those people, the ones
in that mob, every night before she goes to sleep!"

The words of a white schoolteacher—incredulous and, by that
time, quite perplexed. As for me, I'd been interested in knowing
how Ruby slept at night (an indicator of her state of apprehension, a
measure of how well she was handling things mentally), but I hadn't
thought to inquire about what she said or even thought each night
before falling off.

When I finally began to take notice of Ruby's churchgoing activities, and those of her parents, I'm afraid I was not very responsive to
what I heard and saw. Ruby was picking up phrases, admonitions,
statements ritually expressed, bits and pieces of sermons emotionally delivered, and using all that in a gesture of obedience. She was
being psychologically imitative. Her parents told her to pray for her
tormentors, even as those parents had been told to do likewise by

their minister, and Ruby said yes, of course. She did what she was told, but did she truly understand what she was doing? Was she not, rather, showing herself to be a particular six-year-old child: scared, vulnerable, not able to read or write, limited cognitively, vulnerable emotionally—holding on for dear life with brave smiles and silence outside and inside school, and with prayers at home?

Was she not, in addition, a poor black child in an extremely hostile southern city neighborhood, grasping at whatever straws came her way—hence her brave avowals of prayerful concern for those who, after all, wanted to kill her and had no reluctance to say so again and again? When I did prod the child a bit, I got this evidence of what I then concluded to be fearful piety: "They keep coming and saying the bad words, but my momma says they'll get tired after a while and then they'll stop coming. They'll stay home. The minister came to our house and he said the same thing, and not to worry, and I don't. The minister said God is watching and He won't forget, because He never does. The minister says if I forgive the people, and smile at them and pray for them, God will keep a good eye on everything and He'll be our protection."

She stopped and seemed positive. I thought I felt some doubt, some uncertainty. I asked her if she believed the minister was on the right track. "Oh, yes," she said; and then came a kind explanation for the benighted, agnostic, Yankee visitor: "I'm sure God knows what's happening. He's got a lot to worry about; but there is bad trouble here, and He can't help but notice. He may not rush to do anything, not right away. But there will come a day, like you hear in church."

She wasn't sure exactly what would happen on that "day." Even the remarks above weren't delivered as a brief sermon, but constitute an assembled collection of terse explications, delivered over an hour or two on a warm, moist spring afternoon in 1961, a terrible time for that American child and, arguably, for her country as well. Was she, with those explanations, whistling in the dark? Was she repeating in rote submission the clichés a long-impoverished and persecuted people had learned to rely upon—the analgesic self-deceptions of those who, through no fault of their own, have never quite learned to think rationally, logically, or, as some of us would put it, "maturely"? How well did she really understand what was happening to her city, to her neighborhood, to herself and her family? Set aside her composure, her pietistic avowals, her quick smiles, and one would find a terror-struck black child just barely in control of herself—or so I thought; and perhaps the same held for her parents.

Meanwhile my wife's skepticism was directed not at Ruby Bridges and her family, but at the kind of inquiry I seemed determined to make. The more I tried to understand the emotional conflicts, the tensions and responses to tensions, the underlying motivations, and the projections and displacements; the more I emphasized the automatic or reflexive behavior of the children we knew, a consequence of their short lives, their lack of education, their limited cognitive development, their inability to handle all sorts of concepts and symbols; the more I read and commented on various developmental points of view, which emphasized stages and phases and periods—and, of course, consigned elementary school children such as Ruby Bridges to the lower rungs of this or that ladder—the more my wife kept pointing to the *acts* of these boys and girls, the *deeds* they managed.

We had come to know an extraordinary range of children and parents. We had come to know, in addition, a group of poor and poorly educated people who, nevertheless, acquitted themselves impressively in pursuit of significant ethical objectives. I think of Rosa Parks, a seamstress, whose decision to sit where she pleased on a Montgomery, Alabama, bus in the middle 1950s preceded the emergence of the so-called civil rights movement and of Dr. King and Ralph Abernathy as leaders of it. I think of the four college youths who, quietly and without publicity (at first), decided to challenge the segregationist laws of Greensboro, North Carolina, in early February 1960. I think of the many black children my wife and I came to know, in Arkansas and Louisiana and Georgia and Alabama and Mississippi—and of white children, too, who braved awful criticism to befriend them: young leaders of a changing South, young *moral* leaders. Whence that moral capacity, that moral spirit, that moral leadership?

I think it fair to say that a child such as Ruby was in 1961 (aged six, black, southern, of extremely poor background) would not be a likely candidate for the usual kind of moral accolades. She was not "mature." She had, without question, the kinds of cognitive inadequacies we have all come to find important to remember—and connect to the general (academic and social) behavior of the young. She was hardly a candidate for the higher level of performance with respect to moral analysis.

Nevertheless Ruby had a will and used it to make an ethical choice; she demonstrated moral stamina; she possessed honor, courage.

Ruby Bridges came into New Orleans when she was three years old. Her parents had been tenant farmers near Greenville. We would later learn, in the late 1960s and early 1970s, to call such people culturally disadvantaged and culturally deprived: poor folk, poor black folk.

Mr. Bridges was a janitor. Mrs. Bridges, with three small children, took care of those children from morning to night. When she tucked the children in, she went to other homes, got down on her knees, and scrubbed the floors. Then she came home in the middle of the night and was ready for the next morning after just a few hours of sleep. What both parents obviously wanted for their children was a better life than they had.

One day the schoolteacher said to me, "I saw Ruby talking to those people on the street this morning. She stopped and seemed to be talking to the people in the street." Every morning at 8:00 there were at least fifty people there waiting for her, and every afternoon another fifty or seventy-five.

We went to Ruby's home that night, and I asked her, "Ruby, how was your day today?"

She said, "It was okay."

"I was talking to your teacher today and she told me that she asked you about something when you came into school early in the morning."

"I don't remember," Ruby said.

"Your teacher told me that she saw you talking to people in the street."

"Oh, yes. I told her I wasn't talking to them. I was just saying a prayer for them."

"Ruby, you pray for the people there?"

"Oh, yes."

"Really?"

"Yes."

I said, "Why do you do that?"

"Because they need praying for," she answered.

"Do they?"

"Oh, yes."

"Ruby, why do you think they need you to pray for them?"

"Because I should."

"Why?"

"Because I should."

I talked to my wife. "I don't understand why this girl should be praying for them—she's got enough to bear without that."

My wife said, "That's you speaking, but maybe she feels differently." Then my wife asked, "What would you do if you were going through a mob like that twice a day?"

"I can tell you one thing," I answered. "I wouldn't pray for the people who were doing what they're doing to Ruby, or trying to do to Ruby—telling her they were going to kill her, for instance."

My wife constructed the following scenario. "I can just picture you trying to get into the Harvard Faculty Club through mobs.

What would you do if to get into that club in the morning and leave it in the afternoon you had to go through those mobs, and even the police wouldn't protect you?" (They wouldn't, by the way, protect Ruby in New Orleans. Hence the need for federal marshals.)

I assured my wife I would not pray for those people. What we decided I would do was this: First, I would call the police. Ruby couldn't call the police. The police were on the side of the mobs. The second thing I would do is get a lawyer, and fast. Ruby had no lawyer. Ruby had not even been born at the hands of a doctor. The third thing I would do would be to turn immediately on this crowd with language and knowledge. Who are these people, anyway? They are sick. They are marginal, socioeconomically, psychosocially, socioculturally, and psychohistorically. But Ruby did not have the language of sociology or psychology to turn on this crowd. She would not even call them rednecks.

The fourth thing we agreed that I would do, of course, would be to write an article about what I had gone through. Maybe I would even turn it into a book. But Ruby was just learning to read and write.

Ruby and, by the way, many other children we got to know in Little Rock and Clinton, Tennessee, and later in Atlanta, who came from humble homes and who were black people in the South in the 1960s, again and again showed this inclination to pray for their persecutors. What was it? Personal dignity? Prayerful dignity? Once, a couple of weeks after the first time I mentioned it, I again asked Ruby about this praying. "Ruby, I'm still puzzled. I'm trying to figure out why you think you should be the one to pray for such people, given what they do to you twice a day, five days a week."

"Well," she said, "especially it should be me."

"Why you especially?"

"Because if you're going through what they're doing to you, you're the one who should be praying for them." And then she quoted to me what she had heard in church. The minister said that Jesus went through a lot of trouble, and he said about the people who were causing the trouble, "Forgive them, because they don't know what they're doing." And now little Ruby was saying this in the 1960s, about the people in the streets of New Orleans. How is someone like me supposed to account for that, psychologically or any other way?

Here I could get very sophisticated and say that perhaps, although Ruby was saying the words, she did not really understand what they meant. When I tried this observation on my wife, she said, "At least she was saying them. I know a lot of people with a lot more money and power and white skin to boot who wouldn't say it."

"Me included," I said. "I wouldn't."

"That's the point," my wife responded.

So now what was I supposed to do? Call Ruby and her family masochists? Say that they were making statements they didn't comprehend? That they had not studied in college, had not read the implications of what Christ meant when he asked this forgiveness of his tormentors, as interpreted by X, Y, or Z philosopher-theologian?

Later, when I would talk about the mobs in the streets in New Orleans, others would tell me how ignorant they were. They were rednecks, the kind of people who would behave that way. That sounded convincing to me. These poor people in the streets, they were ignorant. They lacked education. It sounded plausible.

The only thing is that one day my wife and I started recalling some of our twentieth-century history. Germany in the 1920s and 1930s did not have a large uneducated population. It was one of the most educated nations in the history of the world. There were great universities in a culture rich and finely textured. It was the nation of Goethe and Schiller and Freud and Einstein. There were impressive scientists, philosophers, social scientists, artists, musicians. Was there ever a more civilized nation? And then Hitler took over in January 1933. If you read German history carefully, you will know that within months, the Nazis had working for them and with them lawyers, doctors, journalists, college professors, and, I regret to say, ministers, theologians, philosophers, and psychiatrists.

But there's little Ruby, who had taken no courses in moral

analysis or systematic ethics. She hadn't read the books we treasure. Yet somehow she walked through that mob praying for those
people. Every day. A year later, when schools had been reluctantly
desegregated, she kept on praying. And quoting from the Bible.
And quoting those statements, those sayings, those stories that Jesus
uttered in Galilee.

I am not about to argue for some kind of anti-intellectualism. But
we do have a lot to learn about what makes for good people in the
living of life. I do not mean "good people" in the sense developmental psychologists mean it. For example, "Let's see, Ruby, we have
some tests here for you. We'll find out about the stage of your moral
development. Answer these various scenarios that we're presenting
to you. What would you do under these circumstances? We will
then grade you and give you a score." These may be very interesting,
hypothetical scenarios. But do we know that someone who does well
at answering those scenarios, put to one in a laboratory, is then going to go out into the street and be honorable in everyday life? This
ought to haunt us.

I remember when I was in college. We would come back to our
rooms and a woman would be there, cleaning our rooms and making our beds. We had a name for these women in the Harvard of the
1950s. We called them biddies.

We never knew the name of the woman who did this for us, because she was just our biddy. She cleaned up after us. And if we were
very thoughtful, some days we might thank her; but I don't want to
remember how many times we never thanked her. And I don't want
to remember how many times we had smashed a beer bottle or two
in the fireplace, knowing that she would clean up after us. After all,
she was being paid to do that. We gave her a big tip at Christmas
time. Never "thank you" or "please." Never any conversation.

At the same time, of course, we were taking courses. Courses, for
instance, in psychology, where we would learn about empathy. You
would get an A in a course by writing for a whole hour on empathy.
But I couldn't tell you the biddy's name. We weren't asked to do that,

because that wasn't part of the curriculum, core or otherwise. It still isn't. I watch my children reading books by great philosophers, and then I wonder, *How can one teach so that what one is teaching engages with a life?*

What does this leave us with now? The great paradox that Christ reminded us about is that sometimes those who are lonely and hurt and vulnerable—*meek*, to use the word—are touched by grace and can show the most extraordinary kind of dignity, and in that sense, inherit not only the next world, but even at times moments of this one. We who have so much knowledge and money and power look on confused, trying to mobilize the intellect, to figure things out. It is not so figurable, is it? These things are mysteries. As Flannery O'Connor said, "Mystery is a great embarrassment to the modern mind."

AFTERWORD

Robert Coles

During the early 1950s, when I was a student at Columbia University's College of Physicians and Surgeons, we who were learning how to figure out what is wrong with whom and why, were graced with the summoning presence of a remarkable teacher, Dr. Yale Kneeland, who taught us how to use our stethoscopes and neurological hammers, and, too, how to interpret X-rays or peer into the eyes and ears of our patients with the help of our ophthalmoscopes and otoscopes—such learning was arduous indeed and, at times, a reminder of how much more we needed to know, and how much longer our apprenticeship would last. One day, as a few of us worked alongside Dr. Kneeland, he asked us to move away from the ward where we were talking and considering the fate of a particularly ailing middle-aged man whose lung cancer our teacher had described as "aggressive and unyielding" (not a usual description we heard from our clinical instructors); a bit surprisingly, our teacher asked us to depart for a nearby small conference room, out of hearing range of the nearby patients. While in that room Dr. Kneeland urged us not only to go after "facts" and a "diagnostic medical analysis," but "language," and to that last word he added this: "We ought try to do justice in our words to the people whose care we are attending—give expression to the particular individuals they

215

have become, here for us to 'cure,' yes, but also here for us to get to know as fellow human beings, as men, women, children who warrant from us not only medical concern, care, but a response as fellow human beings who aim to do justice in our acts, yet also in our words, our ordinary language, not our highfalutin language of so-called expertise, to those who have come to meet us under the adverse circumstances we call an illness, a disease."

Silence, then, not because anything stunning or provocative had been spoken, but because of the forceful emphasis placed on "ordinary language" by Dr. Kneeland through the use of chalk on a nearby blackboard that preceded his comments, his earnestly stated suggestion. He proceeded to elaborate on those two words, and brought up Dr. Chekhov, the physician-writer, and too "a writing doctor across the Hudson," William Carlos Williams, followed by this final remark: "I suppose we could say that how we *think* and *speak* of others matters, even as what we *figure out* and proceed *to do*, also matters." We had been visited with a "bolt of lightning aimed at all of us all in medicine," as my classmate Dick O'Connor (ultimately to be an ophthalmologist) remarked, the first such response to a teacher any of us had made as medical students. Later, we all mused at the significance of that "bolt"—that emphasis on language as, yes, an aspect of our medical work, but also as an aspect of our obligation to do a kind of justice to those fellow human beings whom we called "patients" and, so often, "cases," afflicted with this or that illness.

In a forceful, affecting way, a teacher and physician had moved us to the realm of moral introspection—what "matters" to the patient, and why, as well as what might "matter" to us as his or her "caretaker." There was, soon enough, a long presentation by Dr. Kneeland on "medical ethics," but not one rooted in the abstract, but in an earthy insistence—always his teaching style—on the patient as one suffering, yes, but one weighing life, thinking about its meaning as it unfolds, and then suddenly bringing one up short. Here in a hospital setting was a teaching doctor asking his students to think about the introspective side of things, both the patient's inwardness and the physician's, as together they try to come to terms with a particular life's struggle against a bad turn of fate. At that time, apart from my medical education, I was doing part-time volunteer work in the Catholic Worker soup kitchen run by Dorothy Day and others, across Manhattan from the medical center where I was studying, and I also was spending some time with Dr. William Carlos Williams as he did his house rounds (I'd met him as a college student, having written about and corresponded with him). To be candid now, such activity on my part—working in a soup kitchen, accompanying a writing doctor as he went to see his patients—was getting in the way of my "proper" commitments to medical school life, to the point that I would eventually have to stop, as I was told by a kind but insistent dean, "diverting yourself from school"!

A few years after that part of my medical education, I was fulfilling my responsibilities under the "doctor's draft" law at the time—each of us had to give two years of our time to military service, and I was working at Keesler Air Force Base in Biloxi, Mississippi, as a staff psychiatrist. Soon enough I would be learning about military life, and also about a region of the United States both beautiful to behold but also fraught with considerable social stress and conflict. Soon enough, too, I would encounter Ruby Bridges, one of the four African American children trying to get a first-grade education in a previously all-white school. I happened upon Ruby not by design but by chance—I was on my way to a medical conference in New Orleans, and had to stop because further traffic was impossible due to mobs that had assembled to protest the court-ordered desegregation of the city's schools. My wife, Jane, a high school teacher of history and literature, suggested that I try to meet Ruby and possibly be of help to her, given all the stress she was experiencing; accordingly, I got to spend time with a six-year-old child and her family as they tried hard to put up with a fearful, even dangerous, time in their lives.

Now my work had entered a new pathway—I was getting to learn about how a particular child, Ruby Bridges (and three other youngsters), came to terms with an educational (and social and cultural and racial) crisis, but also one the whole world, so to speak, was watching intently. In no time my psychological inquiry and effort to be of assistance had also become a public matter, and soon enough what I had learned became of interest both to the federal judge, J. Skelly Wright, who had ordered desegregation, and to newspapers and magazines, which tried to convey to the public what was taking place. Now, my words written for medical journals became part of a told story, and now I was asked to write further, and for the public, about what I had seen, heard.

In a sense, the writing that makes up this book is an aftermath to the life I lived in New Orleans (and, later, in Atlanta) as a writing witness to what took place in those cities—and thereafter, as one who continued to try to observe and describe the lives of ordinary men, women, and children, as they struggled to make do, to figure out what was happening, and why, in their lives. Moreover, after writing about Ruby and an elderly lady, Una Anciana, in New Mexico, I was asked by editors of magazines and journals, literary and medical, to respond to other individuals whom I had met or come to know personally: Erik Erikson, Anna Freud, William Carlos Williams, Walker Percy, Bruce Springsteen, Dorothy Day. In sum, as Erik Erikson once said to me, I had become a "wanderer who wanted to see and hear what was happening, and then report back to others—and also one who was wandering through history, choosing to single out certain others": Bonhoeffer, Simone Weil, Dorothea Lange, Flannery O'Connor. Then a pause, and "an afterthought," as Professor Erikson called it, which for me has been not only an enduring memory but a brief, vivid summons of what I have, perhaps, at times unwittingly tried to do: "In the course of your travels (and countless they've been), brief and lengthy, with 'all sorts of conditions of folks' (if you don't mind a religiously linked comment!), there has been a central theme (I hope you don't mind too much my conceptual interpretive inclination!)—the effort on your part to learn what keeps people going, what helps them along, or what gets in their way. You could call it a search for the sustaining in people, for what prods them, inspires them against various odds." Then a final silence on his part, even as today, still in my mind's memory, I hear him telling me how I might understand my working days.

SOURCES

Erik H. Erikson: "Remembering Erik," in *Future of Identity: Centennial Reflections on the Legacy of Erik Erikson*, ed. Kenneth R. Hoover (Lanham, MD: Lexington Books, 2004), 17–21; "Introduction," in Erik H. Erikson, *The Erik Erikson Reader*, ed. Robert Coles (New York: W.W. Norton, 2000), 13–20; excerpts from "Epilogue, Interlude and Prologue," in *Erik H. Erikson: The Growth of His Work* (Booton: Little Brown, 1970), 409–11.

Anna Freud: "Preface," *Anna Freud: The Dream of Psychoanalysis* (Reading, MA: Addison-Wesley, 1992), xv–xxiv; "A Last Conversation with Anna Freud," *New Oxford Review*, April 1992, reprinted in *Harvard Diary: Reflections on the Sacred and the Secular*, vol. 2 (New York: Crossroad, 1997), 102–4; "The Achievement of Anna Freud," *Massachusetts Review* 7, no. 2 (1966): 220.

William Carlos Williams: "The Passaic Stories of William Carlos Williams," *American Poetry Review*, March/April 1975, reprinted as "*Patterson* and the Passaic," in *That Red Wheelbarrow: Selected Literary Essays* (Iowa City: University of Iowa Press, 1988), 304–6; "Dr. Williams at Harvard," *American Poetry Review*, May/June 1983, reprinted as "Dr. Williams at Harvard," in *That Red*

Wheelbarrow, 325–26, 330; "Introduction," in William Carlos Williams, *The Doctor Stories*, comp. Robert Coles (New York: New Directions, 1984), vii–xvi.

Walker Percy: "Introduction," in *Walker Percy: An American Search* (Boston: Little, Brown, 1978), ix–x, xi–xvii; "Shadowing Binx," *Literature and Medicine* 4 (1985), reprinted in *That Red Wheelbarrow*, 103–5, 109.

Dorothy Day: "Remembering Dorothy Day," *New Oxford Review*, April 1981, 5–6; *Dorothy Day: A Radical Devotion* (Reading, MA: Addison-Wesley, 1987), 1–16.

James Agee: "James Agee's Search," *Raritan*, Summer 1983, 133–58.

Flannery O'Connor: "Preface," in *Flannery O'Connor's South* (1980; Athens: University of Georgia Press, 1993), xi–xv; "Flannery O'Connor's Lupus," *Journal of American Medical Association*, September 1980, reprinted as "*The Habit of Being*: Flannery O'Connor's Illness and Collected Letters," in *That Red Wheelbarrow*, 250–54.

Dorothea Lange: *Dorothea Lange: Photographs of Lifetime* (New York: Aperture, 1982), 8–15, 17–26, 29–31, 33–30, 43.

Bruce Springsteen: *Bruce Springsteen's America: The People Listening, a Poet Singing* (New York: Random House, 2003), 12–19, 26–37, 225.

Simone Weil: "Simone Weil: The Mystery of Her Life," *Yale Review*, Winter 1984, 309–20; *Simone Weil: A Modern Pilgrimage* (Reading, MA: Addison-Wesley, 1987), 20–21.

Dietrich Bonhoeffer: "The Making of a Disciple," in Dietrich Bonhoeffer, *Dietrich Bonhoeffer: Writings Selected with an Introduction by
Robert Coles* (Maryknoll, NY: Orbis Books, 1998), 16–27, 37–42.

Una Anciana: *The Old Ones of New Mexico* (Knoxville, TN: Walker
Publishers, 2000), 16–36.

Ruby Bridges: *The Moral Life of Children* (Boston: Atlantic Monthly
Press, 2000), 21–29; "The Inexplicable Prayers of Ruby Bridges,"
Christianity Today, August 9, 1985, 19–20.